These maps tell many stories and show how creative cartography and spatial analytics are being used to create understanding and communicate this understanding effectively. Although some of the maps are simple, most of them are based on large databases and make use of sophisticated GIS tools to manipulate the data.

GIS is becoming a common and popular platform for most organizations. It provides not only visual insights and understanding but also whole new ways for collaboration.

A new pattern of GIS known as Web GIS is emerging. This new paradigm leverages web services and can be used to easily make maps from distributed geographic information of nearly any format. Web GIS is enabling geographic information to be easily shared and directly used in apps that support many operations and run anywhere.

Today, billions of GIS web maps are used to communicate a story. This is creating a new visual language. The result is the reach of GIS is expanding far beyond the domain of GIS professionals.

More people are tapping into the power of GIS and making the kinds of maps and analytics shown in this book.

I want to thank the contributors to *Esri Map Book Volume 33* for sharing their work. Their efforts provide important examples of what's possible and can inspire all of us to do better.

Warm regards,

Jack Dangermond

CONTENTS

SMART SELECT

In this student project, Smart Select is a decision-support tool for commercial real estate investors and others to explore their next investment opportunity in Philadelphia. Without knowing the appropriate price estimate of their own properties, owners find it difficult to provide an asking price and investors are reluctant to consider unfamiliar places. The statistical model in this tool estimates the home price using location factors as predictors so anyone has easy access to find a suggested price for a parcel. By bringing more real-time data and estimation models to the front, more information could be shared in the market to avoid unnecessary price fluctuations.

University of Pennsylvania
School of Design
Philadelphia, Pennsylvania, USA
By Yun Shi

CONTACT
Yun Shi
shiyun_stacy@yahoo.com

SOFTWARE
ArcGIS® for Desktop 10.4

DATA SOURCES
Mapbox, OpenStreetMap

Courtesy of Yun Shi.

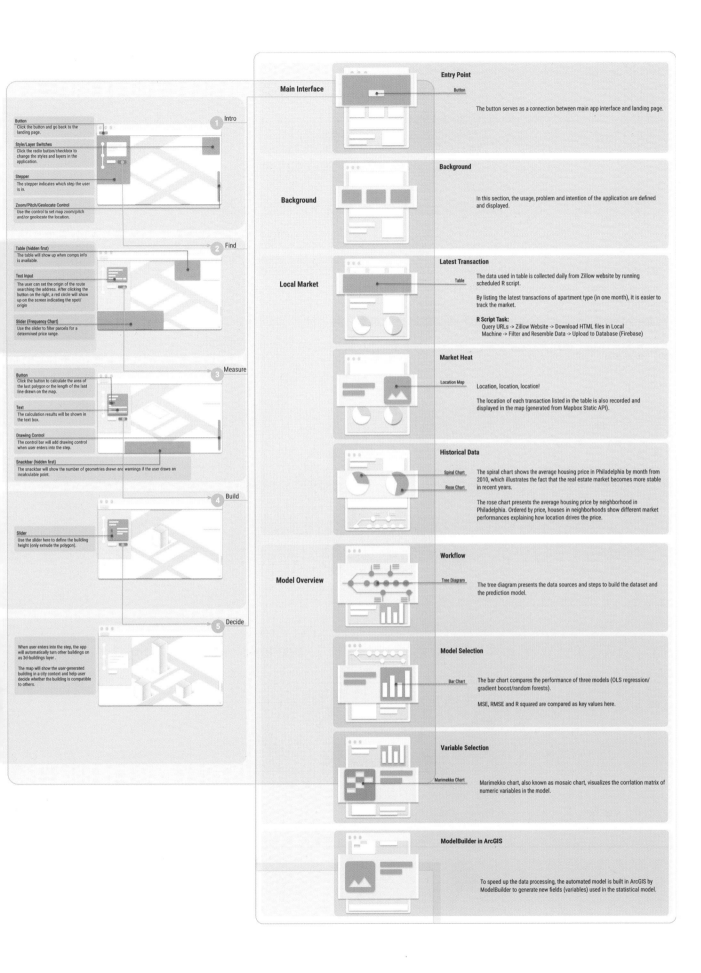

Intro ①

Button
Click the button and go back to the landing page.

Style/Layer Switches
Click the radio button/checkbox to change the styles and layers in the application.

Stepper
The stepper indicates which step the user is in.

Zoom/Pitch/Geolocate Control
Use the control to set map zoom/pitch and/or geolocate the location.

Find ②

Table (hidden first)
The table will show up when comps info is available.

Text Input
The user can set the origin of the route searching the address. After clicking the button on the right, a red circle will show up on the screen indicating the spot/origin

Slider (Frequency Chart)
Use the slider to filter parcels for a determined price range.

Measure ③

Button
Click the button to calculate the area of the last polygon or the length of the last line drawn on the map.

Text
The calculation results will be shown in the text box.

Drawing Control
The control bar will add drawing control when user enters into the step.

Snackbar (hidden first)
The snackbar will show the number of geometries drawn and warnings if the user draws an incalculable point.

Build ④

Slider
Use the slider here to define the building height (only extrude the polygon).

Decide ⑤

When user enters into the step, the app will automatically turn other buildings on as 3d-buildings layer.

The map will show the user-generated building in a city context and help user decide whether the building is compatible to others.

Main Interface

Entry Point
Button

The button serves as a connection between main app interface and landing page.

Background

Background

In this section, the usage, problem and intention of the application are defined and displayed.

Local Market

Latest Transaction
Table

The data used in table is collected daily from Zillow website by running scheduled R script.

By listing the latest transactions of apartment type (in one month), it is easier to track the market.

R Script Task:
Query URLs -> Zillow Website -> Download HTML files in Local Machine -> Filter and Resemble Data -> Upload to Database (Firebase)

Market Heat
Location Map

Location, location, location!

The location of each transaction listed in the table is also recorded and displayed in the map (generated from Mapbox Static API).

Historical Data
Spiral Chart
Rose Chart

The spiral chart shows the average housing price in Philadelphia by month from 2010, which illustrates the fact that the real estate market becomes more stable in recent years.

The rose chart presents the average housing price by neighborhood in Philadelphia. Ordered by price, houses in neighborhoods show different market performances explaining how location drives the price.

Model Overview

Workflow
Tree Diagram

The tree diagram presents the data sources and steps to build the dataset and the prediction model.

Model Selection
Bar Chart

The bar chart compares the performance of three models (OLS regression/gradient boost/random forests).

MSE, RMSE and R squared are compared as key values here.

Variable Selection
Marimekko Chart

Marimekko chart, also known as mosaic chart, visualizes the corrlation matrix of numeric variables in the model.

ModelBuilder in ArcGIS

To speed up the data processing, the automated model is built in ArcGIS by ModelBuilder to generate new fields (variables) used in the statistical model.

WASHINGTON STATE GENDER WAGE GAP

Washington Women in GIS and Techology (UWGT)
Tacoma, Washington, USA
By Stacey Curry, Melissa Hayashida, Tonya Kauhi, Jaclyn Layton, Savanna Nagorski, Rhonda Perozzo, Jennifer Radcliff, Melanie Rogers, and Kaitlin Schrup

WWGT is a professional networking group whose mission is to educate, inspire, mentor, and support women who work in GIS and technology. WWGT created these maps to inform people about the factors that influence the gender wage gap (GWG) and encourage them to get involved. The maps illustrate the percentage of women and men working in STEM (science, technology, engineering, and mathematics) occupations in Washington State as compared to the overall GWG for each county (2011–2015) and the GWG by state for the United States as of 2015.

The GWG is defined as the difference in men's and women's median earnings. The GWG is real, prevalent, and it affects most women. It affects women's age to retire, opportunities for career advancement, opportunities in STEM careers, and ability to pay for school, child care, or living expenses. Women earn on average 80 percent of what men earn and while it is true the GWG is narrowing, women have not yet reached pay equity. The American Association of University Women estimates that fairness in pay will not occur until 2152. The ratification of the Nineteenth Amendment to the US Constitution in 1920 aimed to help women gain social, political, and economic equality and yet women still have an active role to play in educating and supporting wage equity in all forms.

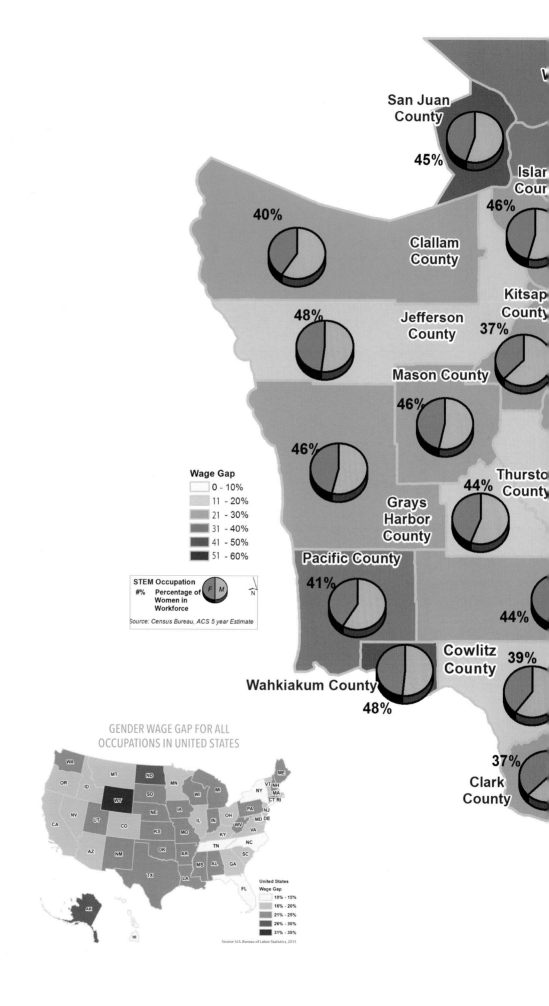

GENDER WAGE GAP FOR ALL OCCUPATIONS IN UNITED STATES

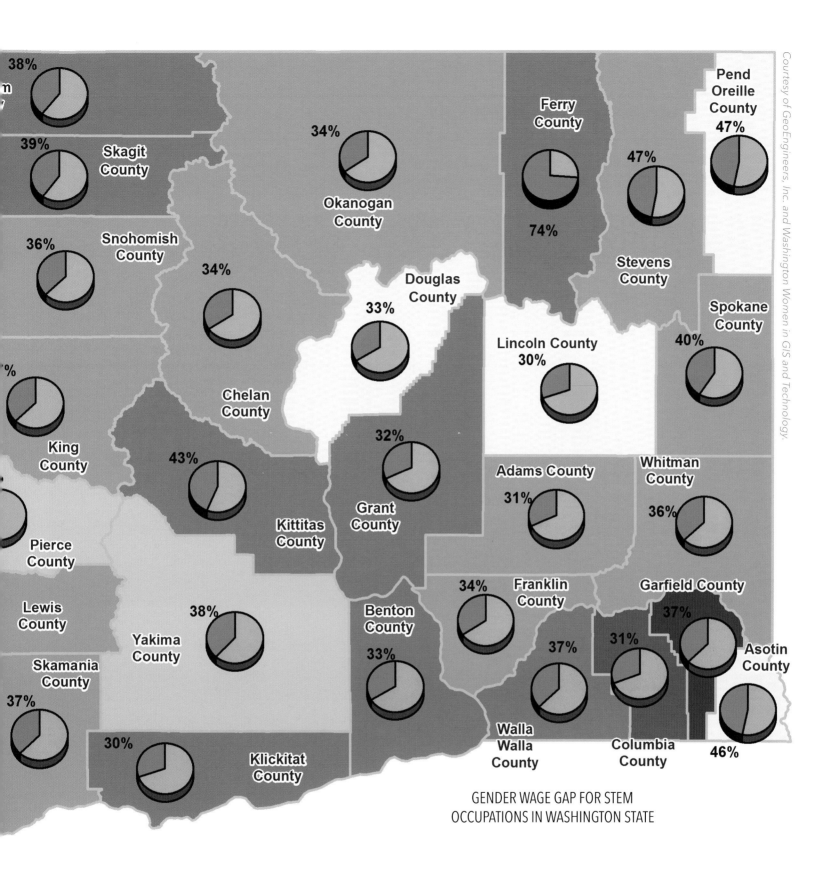

GENDER WAGE GAP FOR STEM
OCCUPATIONS IN WASHINGTON STATE

CONTACT
Tonya Kauhi
tkauhi@portoftacoma.com

SOFTWARE
ArcGIS Desktop 10.1,
Adobe Illustrator CC 2017

DATA SOURCES
National Partnership for Women and Families; US Department of
Commerce, Economics and Statistics Administration; National Women's
Law Center; American Association of University Women; US Census
Bureau; Bureau of Labor Statistics; US Department of Labor

IS YOUR JOB AT RISK OF AUTOMATION?

University of Redlands
Redlands, California, USA
By Jess Chen, Johannes Moenius, and Serene Ong

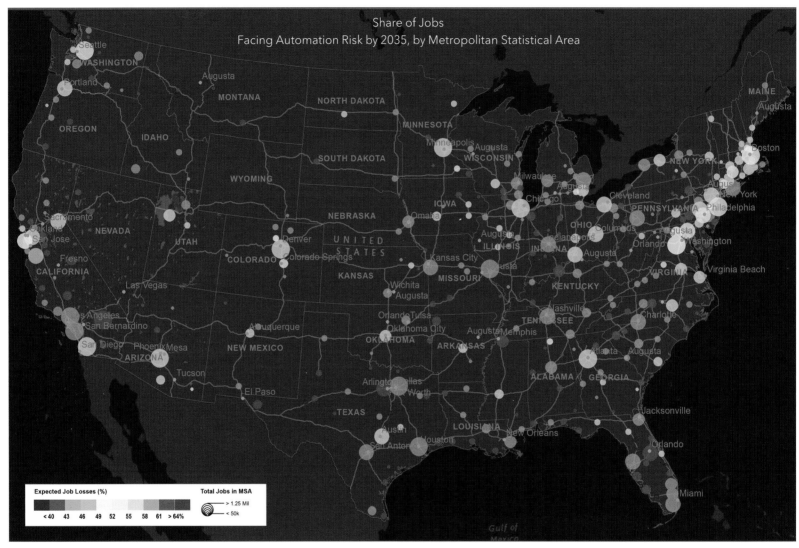

The impact of automation on jobs is likely to be more severe than previously anticipated. Based on recent advances in machine learning and mobile robotics, even non-routine jobs like truck driving, healthcare diagnostics, or even education can be affected (Frey and Osborne, 2013).

According to an Oxford University study, more than 50 percent of all US jobs are susceptible to automation within the next two decades. Robots, which have previously been confined to the manufacturing sector, are now entering the service sector, where 90 percent of American employees work. Some service professions, such as tax preparers, freight agents, and cashiers, face close to certain risk of elimination. Others, such as physicians, social workers, and many education-related jobs, face almost no risk at all.

Job automation will hit certain metropolitan areas significantly harder than others. Low-wage cities like Las Vegas, Nevada; Orlando, Florida; and Riverside–San Bernardino, California currently have the highest shares of jobs that are susceptible to automation. This map illustrates the share of jobs automatable for all 421 metropolitan statistical areas (MSA).

The bubble sizes are proportional to the number of workers employed in the MSA in December 2016. The bubble colors display the share of those jobs that can technically be "automated away" in the next twenty years. As the map shows, almost all large metropolitan areas can lose over 55 percent of their current jobs due to automation. The ones that fare better than others include high-tech centers like Silicon Valley, California, and Boston.

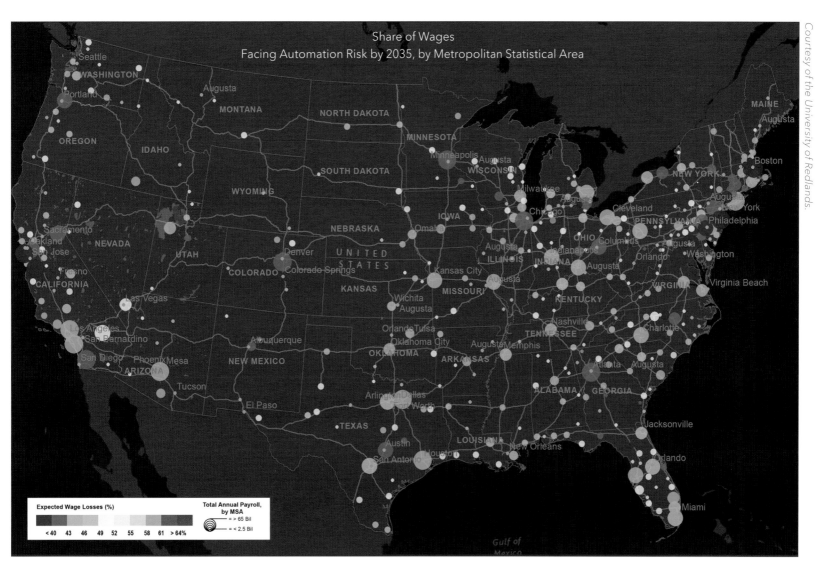

Courtesy of the University of Redlands.

Share of Wages
Facing Automation Risk by 2035, by Metropolitan Statistical Area

Expected Wage Losses (%)

< 40   43   46   49   52   55   58   61   > 64%

Total Annual Payroll, by MSA

= > 65 Bil
= < 2.5 Bil

The map above illustrates the share of jobs automatable for all 421 metropolitan statistical areas (MSAs). The bubble size shows the number of workers employed in the MSA in 2016. The bubble color shows the share of those jobs that can technically be "automated away" in the next 20 years. Almost all large metropolitan areas can lose over 55% of their current jobs due to automation. The ones that fare better than others include high-tech centers like Silicon Valley and Boston

CONTACT
Serene Ong
song@iseapublish.com

SOFTWARE
ArcGIS Desktop 10.3.1

DATA SOURCES
US Bureau of Labor Statistics, Frey, C.B., and Osborne, M.A., 2017. "The Future of Employment: How Susceptible Are Jobs to Computerisation?" *Technological Forecasting and Social Change* 114: 254-280

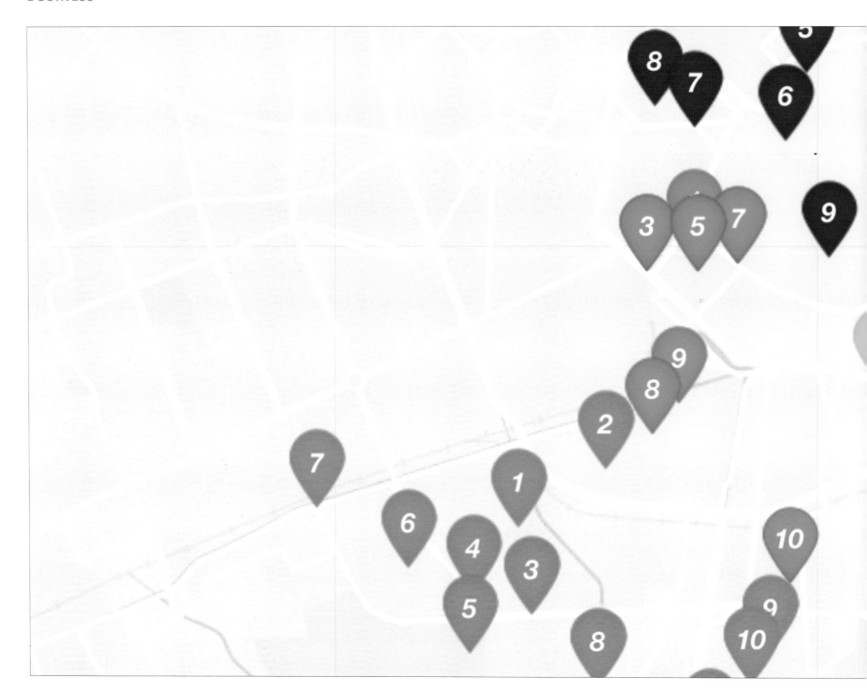

MOBYPLANNER® PLATFORM

MobyPlanner
Milano, Italy
By Marco Cadario

MobyPlanner is an Italian startup company that has developed a geospatial agenda optimizer to help on-the-go employees. The main goal of the product is to solve, with a single click, the complexities that happen when the user's schedule is layered with travel requirements in an urban environment.

The larger map displays employees, workloads, determined by an automatic planning algorithm. The algorithm considers several rules including: employees' skills, events priority and travel time required to reach the appointments on time.

Courtesy of MobyPlanner.

This map is a part of the user's dashboard, where users can interact with the daily schedule by simply dragging and dropping the events on it.

The other image shows how each employee views the daily schedule on MobyPlanner Platform's mobile app. Each pin represents an event whose color depends on delays or overlaps.

CONTACT
Marco Cadario
marco.cadario@mobyplanner.com

SOFTWARE
ArcGIS® Online Rest API

DATA SOURCE
MobyPlanner

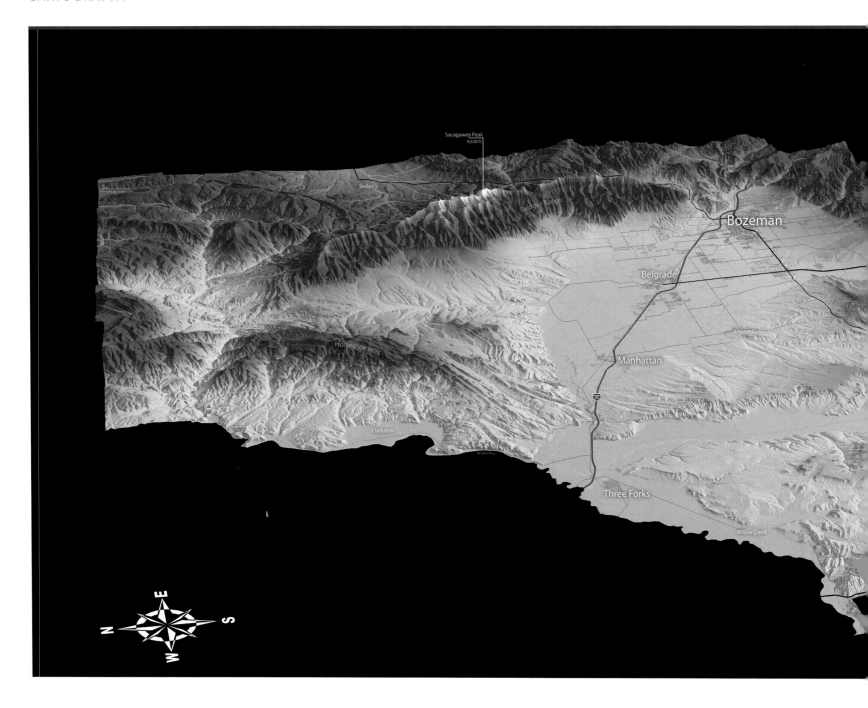

A PERSPECTIVE VIEW OF GALLATIN COUNTY, MONTANA

Gallatin County
Bozeman, Montana, USA
By Frank L. Dougher

Twenty years after Montana State University's Geographical Information Analysis Center produced the first 3D perspective map of Gallatin County, Montana, the county's GIS department revisited the concept and produced a fresh perspective view of the county.

Now viewed from a perspective above the headwaters of the Missouri River, this hypsographic map provides an excellent view of the Gallatin Valley, the mountain ranges that surround it, and the rivers and streams that feed it. The east-skewed orientation of the map provides a drainage-centric perspective of the river and stream systems of Gallatin County. The map also provides a viewshed from the western lowlands to the eastern and southern highlands, and gives the user a more accessible

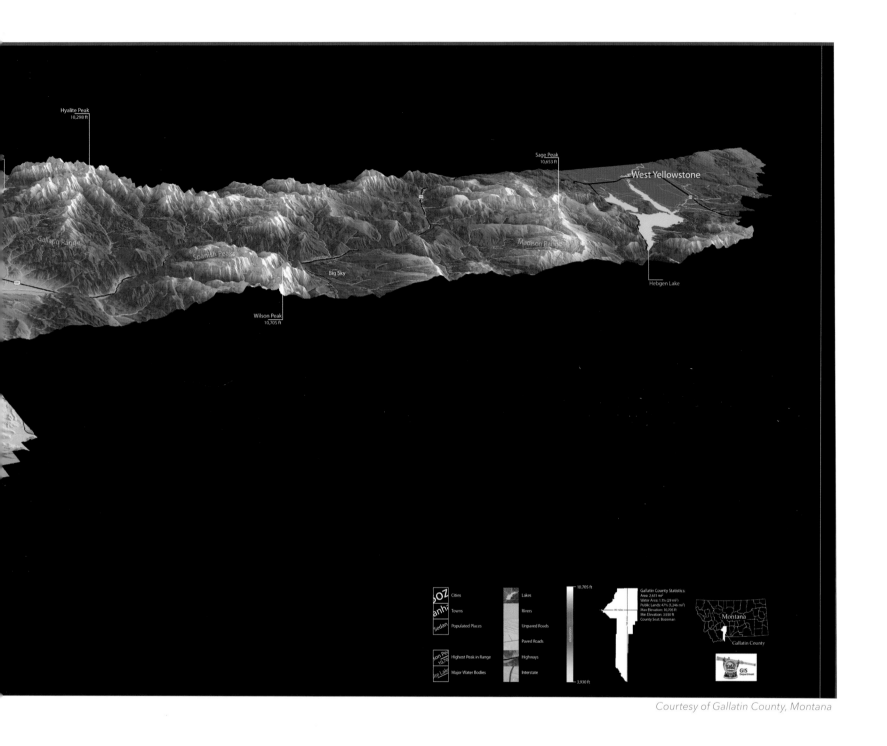

Hyalite Peak
10,298 ft

Sage Peak
10,653 ft

West Yellowstone

Gallatin Range

Spanish Peaks

Madison Range

Big Sky

Hebgen Lake

Wilson Peak
10,705 ft

Cities

Towns

Populated Places

Highest Peak in Range

Major Water Bodies

Lakes

Rivers

Unpaved Roads

Paved Roads

Highways

Interstate

10,705 ft

3,930 ft

Gallatin County Statistics:
Area: 2,631 mi²
Water Area: 1.1% (29 mi²)
Public Lands: 47% (1,246 mi²)
Max Elevation: 10,705 ft
Min Elevation: 3,930 ft
County Seat: Bozeman

Montana

Gallatin County

GIS
Department

Courtesy of Gallatin County, Montana

orientation for reading a map of a county that is more than twice as long on the north-south axis as it is east to west. The mountain ranges that define Gallatin County's landscape are named, along with the highest peaks in the county for each range.

CONTACT
Frank L. Dougher
frank.dougher@gallatin.mt.gov

SOFTWARE
ArcGIS Desktop, GIMP,
Adobe Illustrator

DATA SOURCES
US Geological Survey,
Gallatin County GIS

PATTERNS IN ARCTIC SHIPPING

These maps depict the results of a large space-time analysis of Arctic Automated Identification System (AIS) shipping points from September 2009 to December 2016. Wood Hole Research Center ,in collaboration with the Fletcher School at Tufts University, is working with the longest available record of satellite Automated Identification System ship-tracking data for the Arctic. The dates of the time series run from September 1, 2009 to December 31, 2016. The dataset includes information for all types of ships including type A/big ships such as oil tankers and cargo ships, and type B/small ships, such as fishing vessels and local ferries.

The purpose of this analysis is to support the next Arctic Marine Shipping Assessment and sustainable development of the Arctic. Woods Hole Research Center was also able to map every single ship interacting with sea ice throughout the time series by matching the space and time resolution of the National Snow and Ice Data Center Sea-Ice extent data. Initial results indicate a large jump in the number of type B ships in the Arctic and a mean center shift in overall shipping activity by nearly 300 kilometers to the north and east.

Woods Hole Research Center
Falmouth, Massachusetts, USA
By Greg Fiske

CONTACT
Greg Fiske
gfiske@whrc.org

SOFTWARE
ArcGIS® Pro 2.0

DATA SOURCE
SpaceQuest

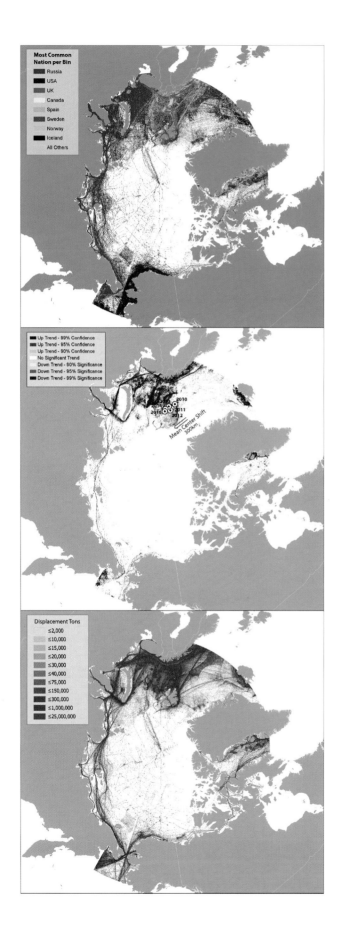

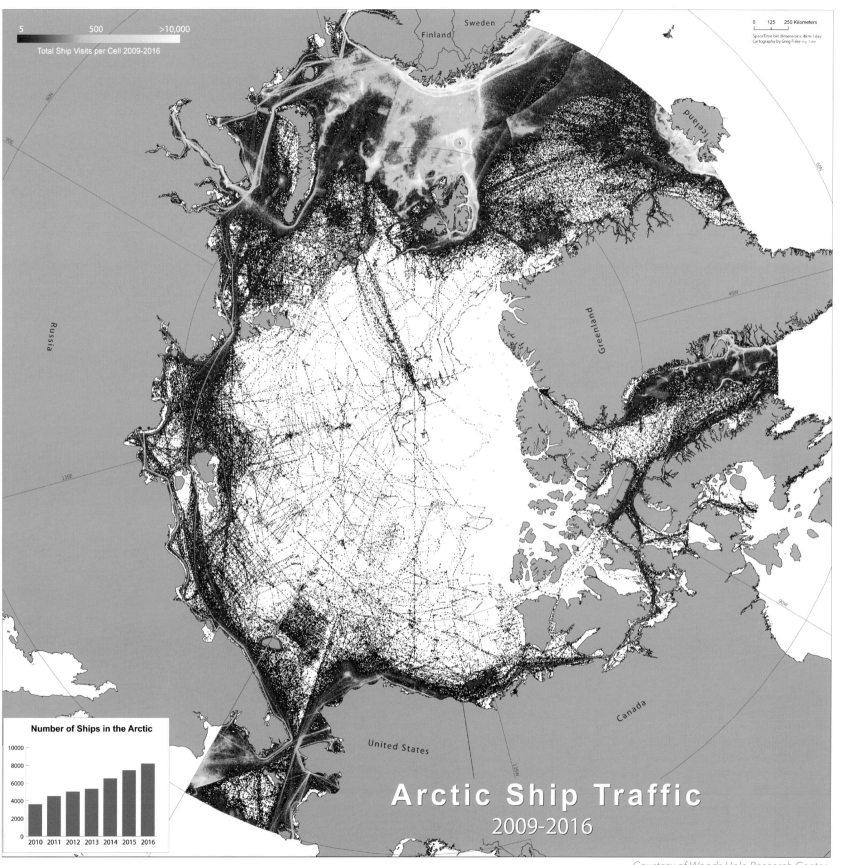

Total Ship Visits per Cell 2009-2016

5   500   >10,000

Sweden
Finland
Iceland
Russia
Greenland
Canada
United States

0   125   250 Kilometers

SpaceTime bin dimensions: 4km-1day
Cartography by Greg Fiske

Number of Ships in the Arctic

Arctic Ship Traffic
2009-2016

Courtesy of Woods Hole Research Center.

ESTIMATING ENVIRONMENTAL QUALITY BY PEER GROUP

The environment is important to human health but environmental data can be difficult to access and use. The Environmental Burden Index (EBI) was created to facilitate environmental health and justice research by making environmental data easier to use and visualize. The EBI aggregates multiple datasets to estimate relative environmental quality at the census-tract level using a unique environmental peer grouping method.

Ranking data by environmental peer groups allows the index to identify tracts with the highest environmental burden relative to other tracts within the same land-cover category rather than just those with the highest level of development. The use of peer groups controls for correlations between urbanicity and environmental data and provides a more accurate estimate of relative environmental quality. EBI estimates are not proxies for exposure and are not related to specific health risks. Data should not be used to support cumulative risk assessment or other analyses requiring specific exposure estimates.

Centers for Disease Control and Prevention
Atlanta, Georgia, USA
By Jessica Kolling, Ian Dunn,
and Brian Lewis

CONTACT
Ian Dunn
lmq8@cdc.gov

SOFTWARE
ArcGIS for Desktop 10.3.1, ArcGIS Pro 1.3,
Inkscape 0.91

DATA SOURCES
Centers for Disease Control and Prevention, Environmental Health Tracking Program; US Environmental Protection Agency, Facility Registry Service; TomTom; US Multi-Resolution Land Characteristics Consortium; National Land Cover Database; US Census Bureau

EBI Rankings

Lowest **Burden** Highest

Urban
Developed - High

Developed - Medium

Developed - Low

Developed - Open

Rural
Forest

Planted/Cultivated

Herbaceous

Shrubland

Wetlands

Water/Barren

0.00 **Index Values** 0.9 1.00
Top 10%

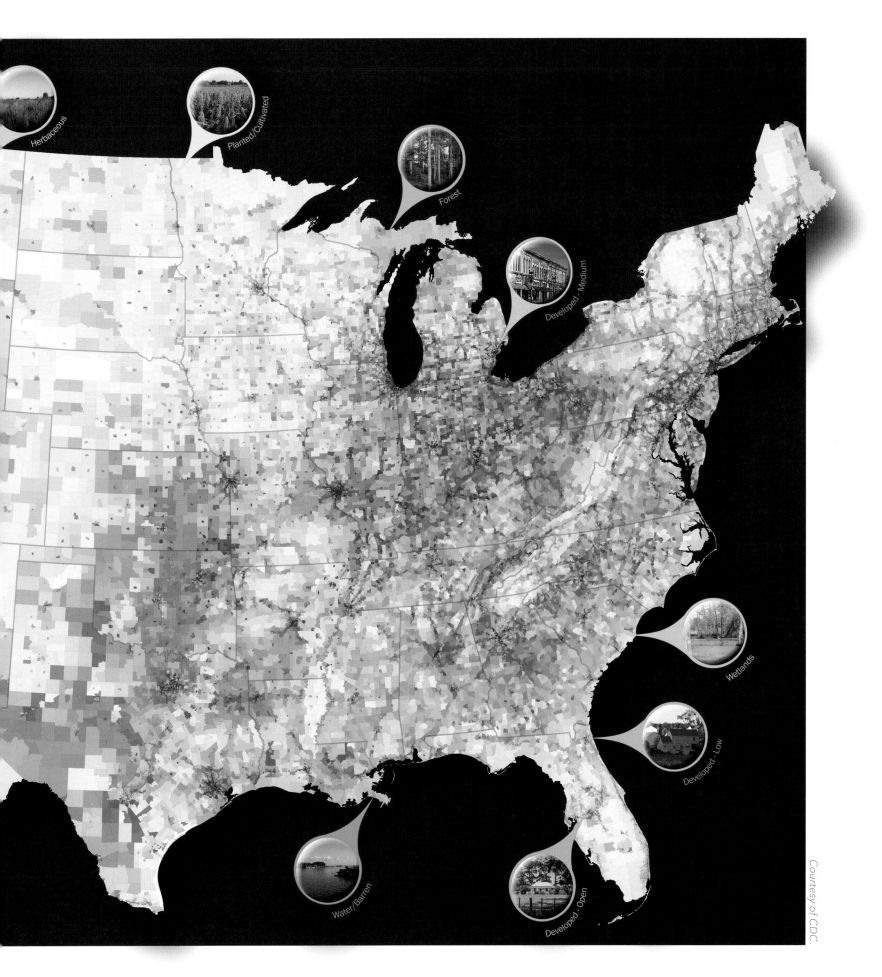

Herbaceous

Planted/Cultivated

Forest

Developed - Medium

Wetlands

Developed - Low

Water/Barren

Developed - Open

ORLANDO AND VICINITY

Orlando, Florida, is a vast urban and suburban region built around innumerable lakes. Wayfinding may involve a lot of circuitous pathways to keep out of the water. Maps.com's comprehensive street map of Orlando was designed for residents, visitors, and tourists in need of direction. The map includes the interstate and highway grid, as well as all city streets, for access to every part of the area. A wide array of key points of interest such as schools, parks, shopping areas, and golf courses are featured.

In addition, public services such as fire and police stations, post offices, libraries, and airports are noted. All these points of interest are indexed for ease of discovery by people exploring the area. Originally designed as a folded street map for drivers, it can also be produced as a flat wall map for businesses. Pastel hues delineate the many cities and towns that make up the greater Orlando landscape, and unincorporated areas are named, all of which also make the map useful as a planning tool for government, or for emergency management.

Maps.com
Santa Barbara, California, USA
By Maps.com

CONTACT
John Glanville
John.Glanville@maps.com

SOFTWARE
ArcGIS Desktop 10.3,
Adobe Illustrator CC

DATA SOURCES
Orange County government,
Seminole County government

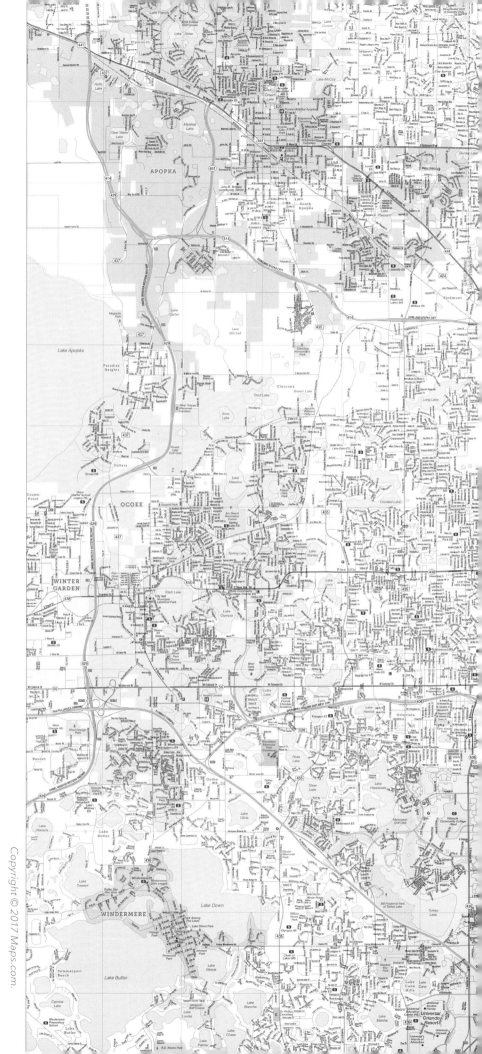

TEXAS RECREATION MAP

The Texas Recreation Map is the first map product to show the real richness of recreation potential in the Lone Star State. The map features land cover (forest, grassland, cropland, and wetland), extensive highway detail, point-to-point mileages, public land ownership, recreation sites, and myriad roadside attractions.This map is offered as two commercial folded-map titles with matching scales for the eastern and western halves of Texas. Both products have regional recreation listings that include national parks and monuments, forests and refuges, state parks and natural areas, boating and fishing access points, natural wonders, historic sites, campgrounds, RV parks, and more.

Benchmark Maps
Santa Barbara, California, USA
By Benchmark Maps

CONTACT
Ryan Reid
Ryan@benchmarkmaps.com

SOFTWARE
ArcGIS Desktop, Adobe Illustrator,
Adobe Photoshop

DATA SOURCES
Texas Department of Transportation, OpenStreetMap, PADUS 1.3, US Fish and Wildlife Service, US Department of Agriculture Forest Service, Texas Parks and Wildlife Department, US Bureau of the Census, Geographic Names Information System, TIGER/Line, Mexico National Institute of Statistics and Geography, field-checked data

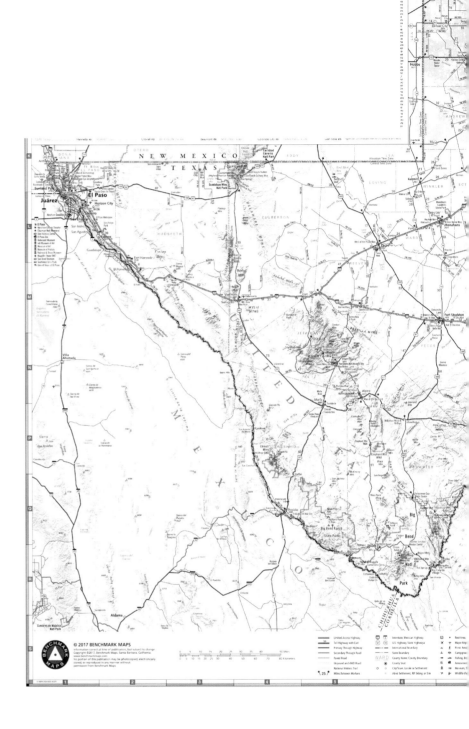

21

NEW YORK STATE WALL MAP

Maps.com's wall map of New York State is part of a fifty-state collection produced for business, education, planning, or decorative use. The map defines the state's constituent counties by use of soft pastel hues behind an extensive roadway system. These interstate and highway networks are shown extending to all of New York's surrounding states and Canadian provinces. A framework of light gray unnamed main roads demonstrates the urban extent of major cities. Each county and county seat are named, and water features are broadly labeled.

With these features, the map is particularly useful for business applications such as defining sales territories and organizing delivery routes. The county and water labels enhance the map's utility as a classroom aid, and the overall design makes it an appealing display on the wall of any proud New Yorker.

Maps.com
Santa Barbara, California, USA
By Maps.com

CONTACT
John Glanville
John.Glanville@maps.com

SOFTWARE
ArcGIS Desktop 10.3,
Adobe Illustrator CC

DATA SOURCE
Maps.com

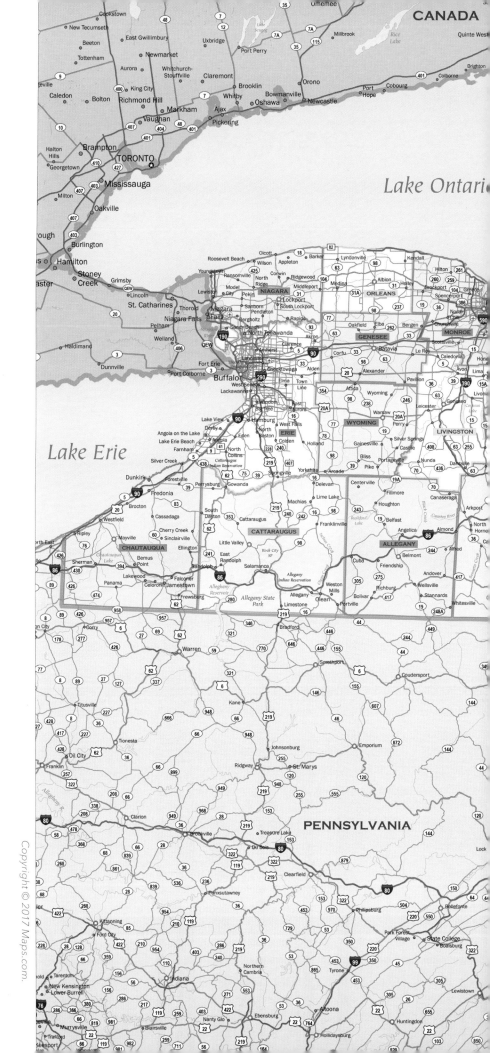

23

COUNTY OF LOS ANGELES SOLAR MAP

Southern California is popularly known for being sunny and this renewable energy source can be captured through solar panel installations. The Los Angeles County Energy and Environmental Service has developed a solar map app (solarmap.lacounty.gov) to bring new visualization and analysis tools for residents and businesses interested in "going green" to reduce energy costs and carbon emissions.

The app provides detailed rooftop and parking lot shading visualization for panel placements based on suitable area and it also provides graphical calculators detailing costs, savings, and payback for solar systems. Users can visually inspect rooftops and parking lots using high-resolution imagery from Los Angeles Region Imagery Acquisition Consortium, access the site and solar data on any device, and generate property-level solar reports.

This map is centered in a small area in the city of Downey, where it shows solar potential for every rooftop and solar carport (parking lots). The Area Solar Radiation tool in ArcGIS Desktop was used to derive incoming solar radiation using a combination of a digital elevation and surface model. Red color dots (for rooftops) and squares (for carports) show excellent locations or conditions to capture sunlight, yellow indicates fair conditions, and blue indicates areas that are not advisable due to shading from adjacent trees and structures.

County of Los Angeles Internal Services Department
Downey, California, USA
By Christine Lam

CONTACT
Christine Lam
CLam2@isd.labounty.gov

SOFTWARE
ArcGIS Desktop

DATA SOURCES
Los Angeles Region Imagery Acquisition Consortium, County of Los Angeles Enterprise GIS Repository

Solar Carport Points

- Excellent (>3.8 kWh/m²/day)
- Good (2.8 to 3.79 kWh/m²/day)
- Fair (2.3 to 2.79 kWh/m²/day)
- Poor (1.9 to 2.29 kWh/m²/day)
- Not Advisable (<1.9 kWh/m²/day)

Solar Rooftop Points

- Excellent (>4.9 kWh/m²/day)
- Good (4.0 to 4.99 kWh/m²/day)
- Poor (3.3 to 4.0 kWh/m²/day)
- Not Advisable (<3.3 kWh/m²/day)

Units are kilowatt hours per square meter per day.

PROTECTING REGIONS OF THE ARCTIC

Many governments and nongovernmental organizations are collaborating to protect the marine ecosystems of the Arctic in the face of climate change and increasing pressure from industry. This task is complicated by the different designations of protection as well as by the numerous governing bodies that have created these designations.

Marine Protected Areas of the Arctic are being explored to determine their current state of protection within the larger Important Marine Areas included in this analysis. Different approaches were used to identify the ecologically important marine areas and these areas are not wholly protected. The entire central Arctic Ocean sea ice is an ecologically important area but was omitted from the analysis because there are no protective measures in place for that region.

Portland State University
Portland, Oregon, USA
By Gabriel Rousseau and Kyle Lempinen

CONTACT
Gabriel Rousseau
gwr@pdx.edu

SOFTWARE
ArcGIS Desktop 10.3, Adobe Illustrator, Adobe Photoshop

DATA SOURCES
Arctic Council, Bureau of Ocean Energy Mangement, Convention on Biological Diversity, Climate Works, Esri, Fisherines and Oceans Canada, International Union or Conservation of Nature, MPAtlas, NASA, National Geographic Society, National Snow and Ice Data Center, Natural Earth, National Oceanic and Atmospheric Administration, Natural Resources Defense Council, US Geological Survey, World Database on Protected Areas

Courtesy of Gabriel Rousseau.

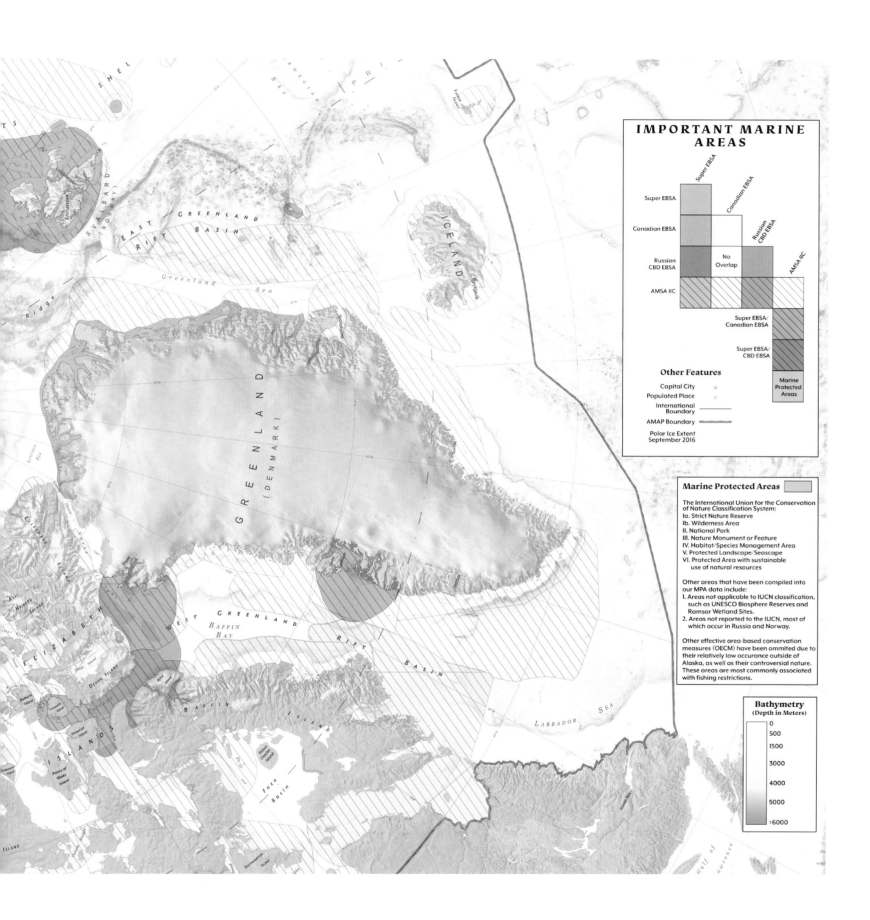

IMPORTANT MARINE AREAS

	Super EBSA	Canadian EBSA	Russian CBD EBSA	AMSA IIC
Super EBSA				
Canadian EBSA				
Russian CBD EBSA		No Overlap		
AMSA IIC				

Super EBSA/
Canadian EBSA

Super EBSA/
CBD EBSA

Marine
Protected
Areas

Other Features

Capital City ⊚

Populated Place ∘

International
Boundary ――――

AMAP Boundary ▨▨▨▨▨▨▨

Polar Ice Extent
September 2016

Marine Protected Areas ▨

The International Union for the Conservation
of Nature Classification System:
Ia. Strict Nature Reserve
Ib. Wilderness Area
II. National Park
III. Nature Monument or Feature
IV. Habitat/Species Management Area
V. Protected Landscape/Seascape
VI. Protected Area with sustainable
    use of natural resources

Other areas that have been compiled into
our MPA data include:
1. Areas not applicable to IUCN classification,
   such as UNESCO Biosphere Reserves and
   Ramsar Wetland Sites.
2. Areas not reported to the IUCN, most of
   which occur in Russia and Norway.

Other effective area-based conservation
measures (OECM) have been ommited due to
their relatively low occurance outside of
Alaska, as well as their controversial nature.
These areas are most commonly associated
with fishing restrictions.

Bathymetry
(Depth in Meters)

0
500
1500
3000
4000
5000
>6000

27

SWAMPED: PROPOSING WETLAND RESTORATION

Wetlands provide many functions including flood protection, nutrient and sediment pollution mitigation, carbon sequestration, and wildlife habitat. However, from the advent of tile drainage through the era of "fencerow-to-fencerow" agricultural policy, draining wetlands for agriculture was common. Unfortunately, highly segmented wetlands provide substantially fewer benefits than well-connected wetland systems. Plus, agricultural areas that are losing tons of soil each year may be better off serving as agricultural pollutant remediation sites.

This student project aimed to predict areas where wetland restoration would be of most benefit, through restoring areas that were previously drained, prioritizing areas of high soil loss, and maintaining connectivity with existing wetlands. This map shows potential wetland restoration corridors in three sub basins of the Tallahatchie watershed, about 25 miles east of the Mississippi River. These 200-meter-wide paths connect existing wetlands while prioritizing paths that cross through agricultural land with high calculated soil loss, according to a spatial Revised Universal Soil Loss Equation model. Of course, these fixed-width paths may not be the ideal restoration model, but this map serves as a proof of concept in prioritizing wetland restoration according to high agricultural soil loss and connectivity between wetlands.

Tufts University
Medford, Massachusetts, USA
By Elisabeth Spratt

CONTACT
Elisabeth Spratt
elisabethspratt@gmail.com

SOFTWARE
ArcGIS Desktop 10.4.1

DATA SOURCES
SSURGO, National Wetlands Inventory, Cropscape

Courtesy of Elisabeth Spratt and Tufts University.

water bodies
existing wetlands
best restoration paths
RUSLE-estimated soil loss
Value
High : 35.5 tons/acre/year
Low : 0.1 tons/acre/year

NATURE-BASED SOLUTIONS TO CLIMATE CHANGE

Conservation International (CI)
Arlington, Virginia, USA
By Mariano Gonzalez-Roglich, Jenny Hewson,
Karyn Tabor, Tracy Tien, Leo Saenz, Steve Panfil,
Kellee Koenig, and Dave Hole

Nature-based solutions to climate change, including REDD+, Ecosystem-based Adaptation, and Blue Carbon, have been widely promoted within the United Nations Framework Convention on Climate Change (UNFCCC) policy discussions and in other national and international forums as providing both climate change mitigation and adaptation benefits, alongside a range of other social and biodiversity co-benefits. They have also been highlighted by many countries as part of their Nationally Determined Contributions to reducing climate change impacts.

However, investments in nature-based solutions are grossly insufficient, totaling less than 3 percent of global climate finance, according to Climate Policy Initiative 2015. Recognizing this imbalance between current investment and the potential of nature to deliver mitigation and adaptation benefits, Conservation International (CI) implemented a project to identify which regions of the world offer the greatest scope for the implementation of nature-based solutions for mitigation and biodiversity benefits. CI explored the spatial synergies between REDD+ and biodiversity benefits to identify global opportunities for investment based on the magnitude of mitigation outcomes, together with the level of biodiversity cobenefits, and current/likely future threats to these areas.

CI used a multi-criteria evaluation approach to develop indicators that could be used independently to prioritize investments, or integrated to identify synergies between REDD+ and biodiversity; the analysis included all forest located in developing nations.

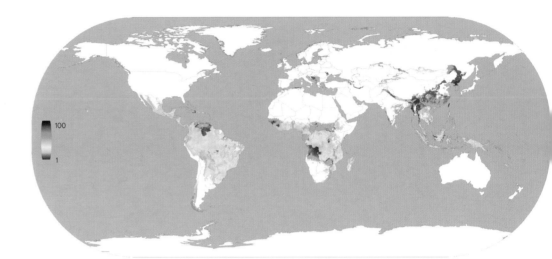

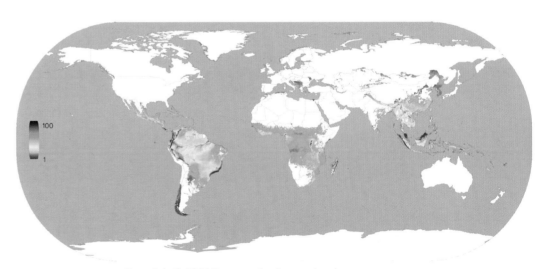

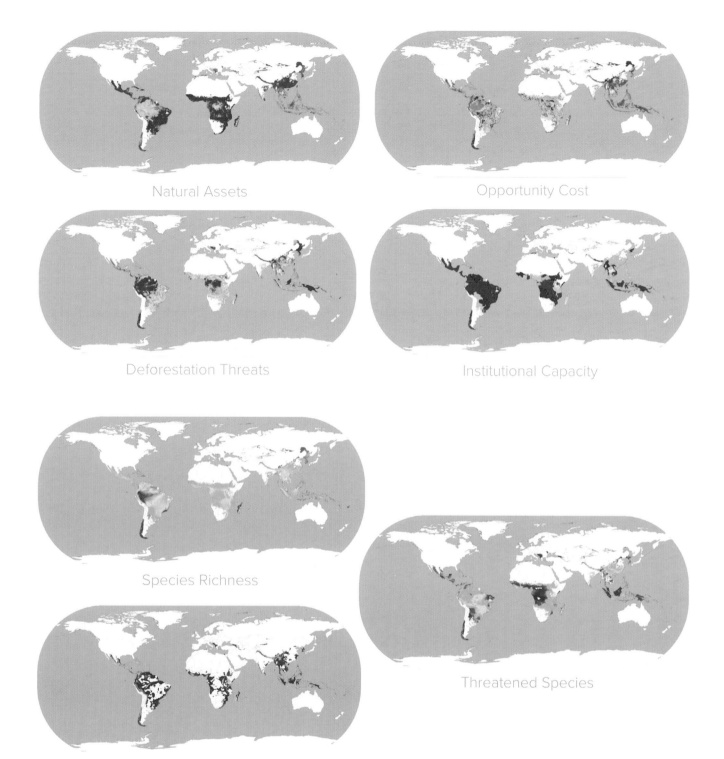

Natural Assets

Opportunity Cost

Deforestation Threats

Institutional Capacity

Species Richness

Threatened Species

Small-ranged Species Richness

CONTACT
Kellee Koenig
kkoenig@conservation.org

SOFTWARE
ArcGIS Desktop 10.5

DATA SOURCES
Climate Policy Initiative, Forest Carbon
Partnership Facility, United Nations
Framework Convention on Climate Change,
Verified Carbon Standard Project Database

CLIMATE RISK IN THE AMAZON BIOME

This map depicts the spatial distribution of the Regional Climate Change Index (RCCI) for the Amazon biome. The RCCI analyzes how temperature and precipitation changes between current and future scenarios will be distributed throughout the biome, taking into account the intrannual temperature and precipitation variability and seasonality. This information is very useful because it helps decision-makers identify which regions will probably endure an increase in the frequency and magnitude of future extreme climate events, such as floods or droughts, and thus plan the development of their territory accordingly.

WWF Colombia
Cali, Valle del Cauca, Colombia
By Johanna Prüssmann, César Freddy Suárez, and Maria Elfi Chaves

CONTACT
Johanna Prüssmann
jprussmann@wwf.org.co

SOFTWARE
ArcGIS Desktop 10.4

DATA SOURCES
Hijmans, R.J., S.E. Cameron, J.L. Parra, P.G. Jones and A. Jarvis. 2005. "Very High Resolution Interpolated Climate Surfaces for Global Land Areas." International Journal of Climatology 25: 1965–1978; WWF; Redparques; UN Food and Agriculture Organization; International Union for Conservation of Nature; UN Environmental Programme; Federal Environment Ministry

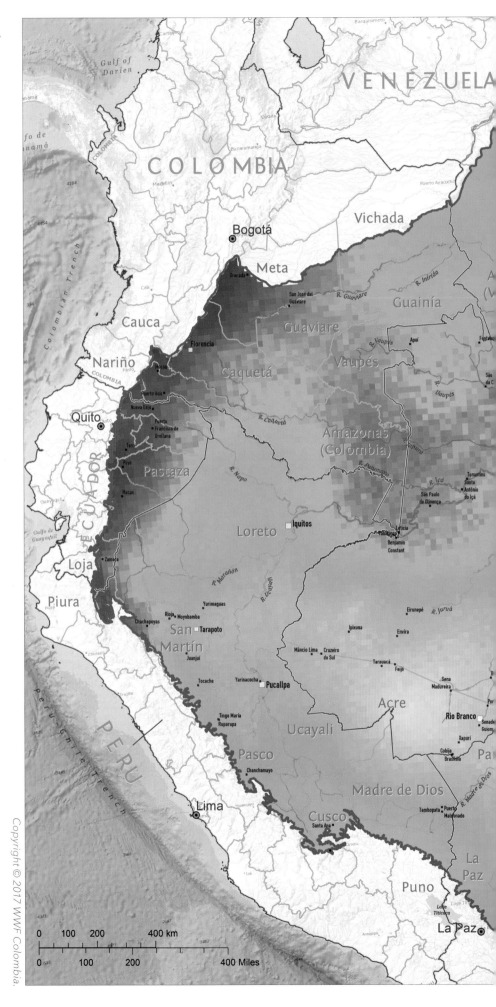

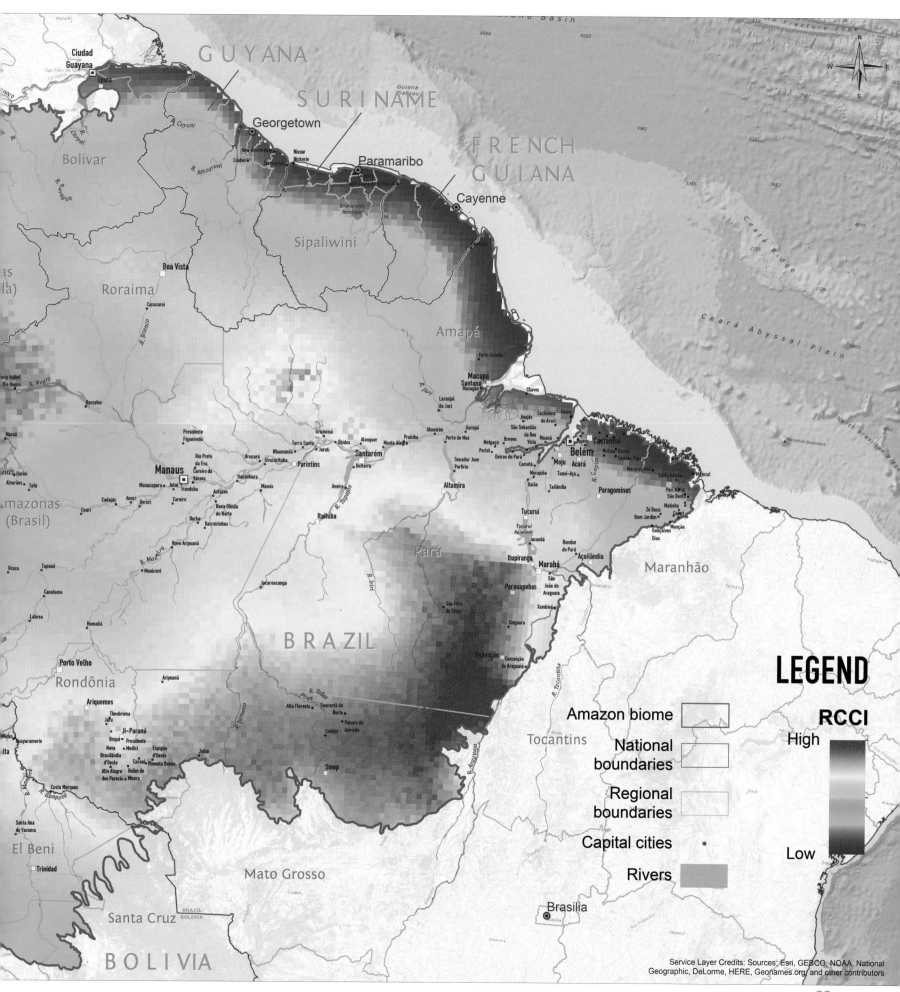

LEGEND

Amazon biome

National boundaries

Regional boundaries

Capital cities

Rivers

RCCI

High

Low

Service Layer Credits: Sources: Esri, GEBCO, NOAA, National Geographic, DeLorme, HERE, Geonames.org, and other contributors

TERRORISM IN SYRIAN CRISIS

This student-produced map identifies terrorism in Syria in 2016. The data was taken from a previous ArcGIS map, a population layer, border layers, and current numbers from the CIA fact book to update the death count. The data helps the reader understand two main things: the complex sides and boundaries of the Syrian civil war, and the death toll from terrorist attacks in each area. For this data, the gas attacks by the Assad regime are not incorporated in the terrorism death toll, and over 90 percent of the groups committing acts of terror were ISIS. The map breaks down each territory (Kurdish, ISIS, regime, and rebel) to show the death toll for each region.

Each region is separated and identified by color, and the death toll is shown through dots that increase in size with more deaths. This information could be useful to many groups, including world governments, defense agencies, and human rights organizations. This information, if interpreted correctly and accompanied by other data such as roads and airports, can help get people out of these areas who are most affected by terrorist attacks.

Loudoun County Public Schools
Science Office
Ashburn, Virginia, USA
By Joshua Toohey

CONTACT
Michael Wagner
Michael.Wagner@lcps.org

SOFTWARE
ArcGIS Desktop 10.4.1

DATA SOURCES
Esri, HERE, DeLorme, Intermap, increment P Corp., General Bathymetric Chart of the Oceans, US Geological Survey, UN Food and Agriculture Organization, National Park Service, National Resources Canada, GeoBase, IGN, Kadaster Netherlands, Ordnance Survey, Esri Japan, METI, Esri China (Hong Kong), swisstopo, MapmyIndia, OpenStreetMap

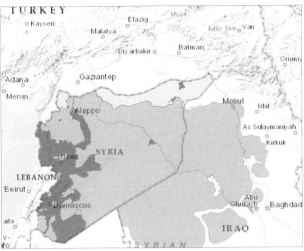

This map shows the current boundaries of all major parties in the Syrian conflict. The boundaries are constantly changing, and can change within a week.

Syria Boundaries

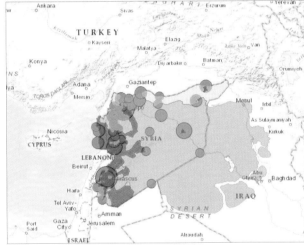

This map reveals the areas where terrorist attacks have occurred, and how many fatalities there have been in those areas due to terrorism. The total body count racks up to 2,266 deaths.

Syria Fatalities Due to Terrorist Attacks

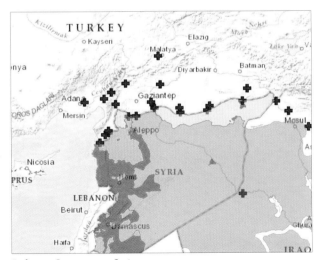

This map shows the locations of refugee camps for Syrian refugees. Most of them are in the north and northeast, around Kurdish and ISIS land.

Refugee Camps near Syria

This regime territory had a total of 1,642 deaths due to terrorist attacks in the past 2 years. This accounts for over 70% of the deaths due to terrorism in Syria.

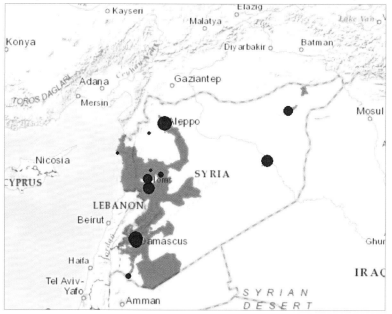

Syria Fatalities Due to Terrorist Attacks in Regime Territory

8% of terrorist deaths in Syria happened in rebel territory, which is the third largest portion, by a large margin.

Syria Fatalities Due to Terrorist Attacks in Rebel Territory

Syrian Fatalities Due to Terrorist Attacks in Kurdish Territory

This least amount of deaths due to terrorism is in the Kurdish territory. Only 92 people have died from terrorism in the past 2 years.

Syrian Fatalities Due to Terrorist Attacks in Isis Territory

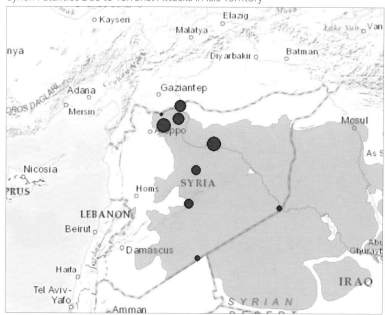

350 people have been killed by terrorism in Isis territory, which makes up 16% of the deaths in Syria due to terrorism

35

SALLY RIDE EARTHKAM: MAPPING STUDENT PHOTOGRAPHS

Sally Ride EarthKAM is a digital camera payload on the International Space Station (ISS) that provides a platform for science, technology, engineering, and mathematics (STEM) outreach and education. Managed by the US Space and Rocket Center and the University of Alabama in Huntsville, this nadir-facing camera system allows K–12 students around the world to control the camera and task it to take photographs of Earth, which they can then download and use in the classroom.

More than 28,000 photograph requests from students in ninety-five countries during ISS Increments 46-51 were collected, georeferenced, and analyzed using a weighted count approach according to the number of times the camera was tasked to take a photograph. The results of this study illustrate patterns about request geographies, such as places of interest for classrooms in different countries and at different grade levels, in addition to demonstrating a GIS workflow for information from a NASA ISS-based camera system. This research was supported under a cooperative agreement with the NASA ISS National Laboratory/JSC, NNJ15GU14A.

US Space and Rocket Center, and
Teledyne Brown Engineering

University of Alabama in Huntsville
Huntsville, Alabama, USA
By Robert Griffin, Jeremy Frost, Tim Klug, Tyler Finley, Scott Harbour, Brion Au, and Sara Graves

CONTACT
Robert Griffin
robert.griffin@nsstc.uah.edu

SOFTWARE
ArcGIS Desktop 10

DATA SOURCES
NASA, Sally Ride EarthKAM

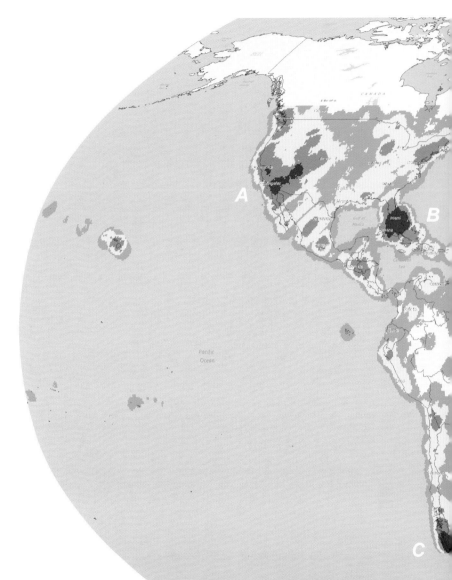

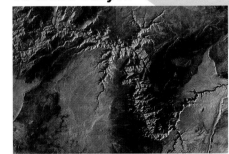

A. Grand Canyon

2016/279/00:15:10 (October 5, 2016)
CCFID 114355 / 50mm lens

B. Tongue of the Ocean

2017/091/21:39:02 (April 1, 2017)
CCFID 134433 / 50mm lens

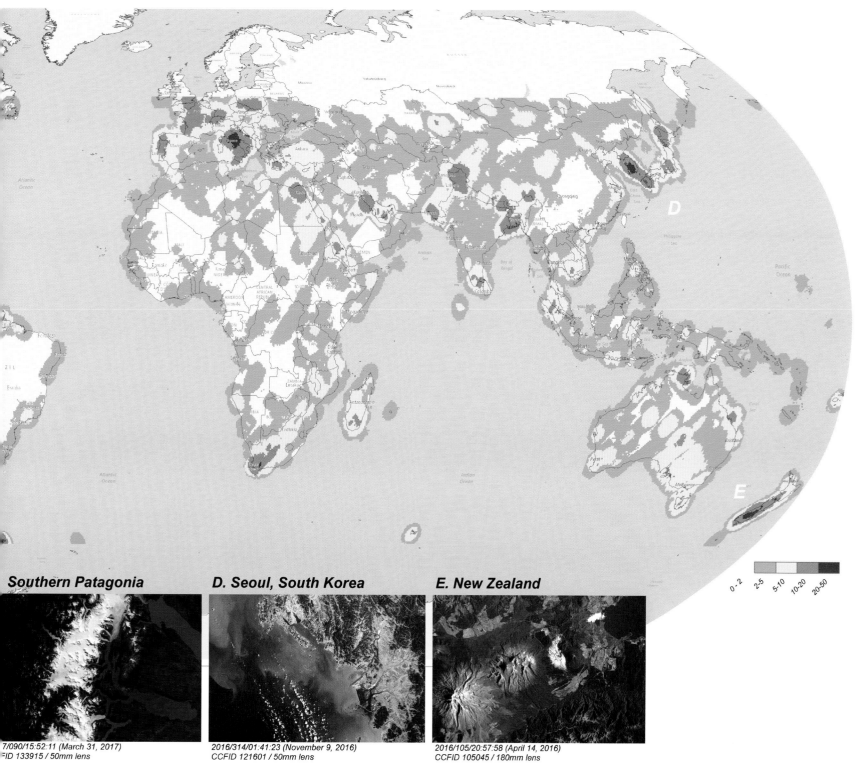

Southern Patagonia

D. Seoul, South Korea

E. New Zealand

7/090/15:52:11 (March 31, 2017)
FID 133915 / 50mm lens

2016/314/01:41:23 (November 9, 2016)
CCFID 121601 / 50mm lens

2016/105/20:57:58 (April 14, 2016)
CCFID 105045 / 180mm lens

0 - 2   2-5   5-10   10-20   20-50

VISUALIZING SCHOOL ENROLLMENT TRENDS

Portland State University
Portland, Oregon, USA
By Richard Lycan and Charles Rynerson

Portland State University provides demographic services to Portland Public Schools. An important part of this service is to explain to school administrators and the public how the demography of the school district is changing. Two measures of change are explained in this display: grade progression ratio and public-school capture rate. The grade progression ratio tracks changes in grade-level cohorts.

For example, 1A shows the progression of the grade KG–02 cohort in 2000 to grade 03–05 in 2003 where it increases from 525 to 532 students, a grade progression a ratio of 1.013. Maps 1B and 1C show a similar computation but using an adapted bandwidth grid mapping for KG–02 for 2000 and 2008. They show a generally similar pattern, but in some areas the grade progression ratios are higher in 2008 than in 2000 confirming that the district is doing a better job of retaining students in these areas.

The public-school capture rate represents the proportion of age-eligible students enrolled in Portland Public Schools. One method to find this ratio is to compare enrollment data obtained from private schools to the total (2) but this data doesn't show where the students live. The Census Bureau's American Community Survey asks whether students are in public or private schools but the sample is small and the estimates are unreliable for small areas (3A, 3B). A better method is to compare the geocoded location of students to age-eligible population from the census (4A, 4B).

CONTACT
Richard Lycan
lycand@pdx.edu

SOFTWARE
ArcGIS Desktop 10.4.1, CrimeStat IV, Microsoft Office Professional Plus 2013, Adobe Illustrator CS6

DATA SOURCES
Portland Public Schools, US Census, American Community Survey, Portland Metro

Grade Progression Ratio

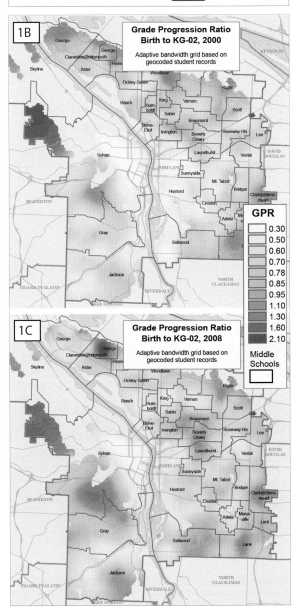

1A

Enrollment History

Year	Grade Level			
	KG-02	03-05	06-08	09-11
2000	525	561	538	501
2003	514	532	546	486
2006	542	511	505	466
2009	643	562	491	454

Enrollment History

Year	Grade Level			
	KG-02	03-05	06-08	09-11
2000	525	561	538	501
2003	514	532	546	486
2006	542	511	505	466
2009	643	562	526	454

Grade Progression Ratio	Ratio to Prior Cohort	Grade Level		
		KG-02	03-05	06-08	09-11
		Births	KG-02	03-05	06-08
GPR			1.013	0.973	0.903

Grade Progression Ratio Birth to KG-02, 2000
Adaptive bandwidth grid based on geocoded student records

Grade Progression Ratio Birth to KG-02, 2008
Adaptive bandwidth grid based on geocoded student records

GPR
0.30
0.50
0.60
0.70
0.78
0.85
0.95
1.10
1.30
1.60
2.10

Middle Schools

Public School Capture Rate

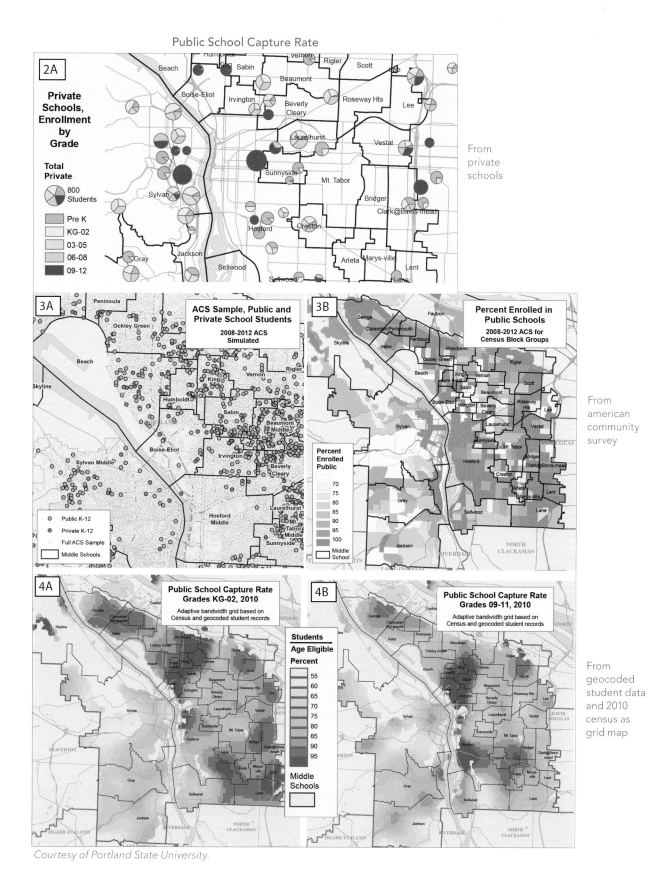

From private schools

From american community survey

From geocoded student data and 2010 census as grid map

Courtesy of Portland State University.

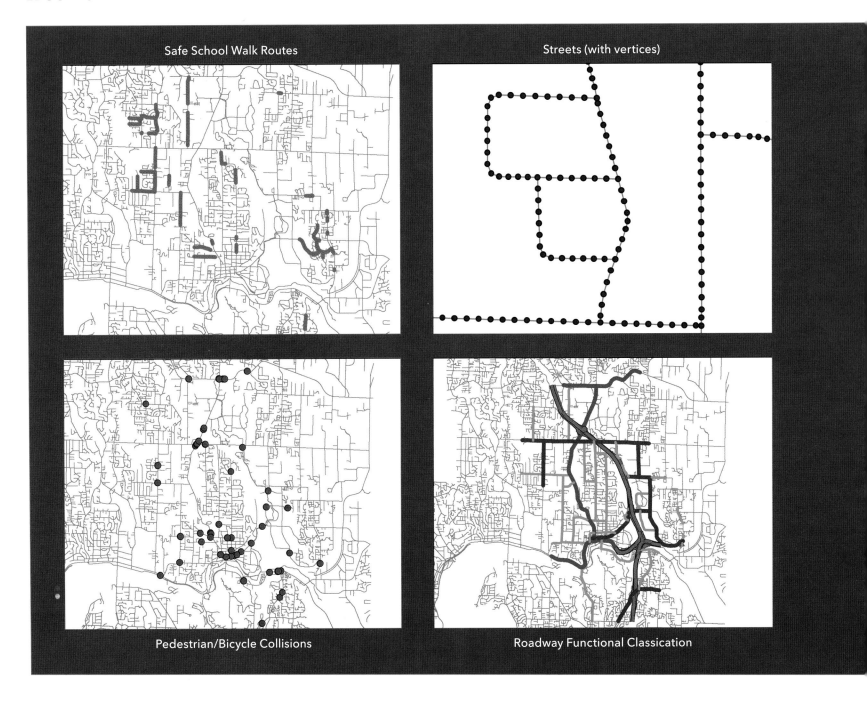

Safe School Walk Routes

Streets (with vertices)

Pedestrian/Bicycle Collisions

Roadway Functional Classication

SAFE SCHOOL WALK ROUTES STUDY

City of Bothell
Bothell, Washington,
USA

By Andy Siegel and
Daryn Brown

In recent years, many cities have responded to the Americans with Disabilities Act by implementing comprehensive programs to bring their sidewalks into compliance. This project consisted of using GIS spatial and statistical analysis to prioritize future projects in high-use public school neighborhoods.

The City of Bothell has 44,000 citizens and is in Washington State's rapidly growing northcentral Puget

Sound region. In November 2016, the Bothell citizens voted for the Safe Streets and Sidewalks Levy. With this funding, the Public Works Department formed a taskforce that identified school needs, determined criteria for the prioritization process, and developed a list of potential sidewalk projects.

The city staff then collaborated to determine the best spatial analysis method and data criteria for calculating

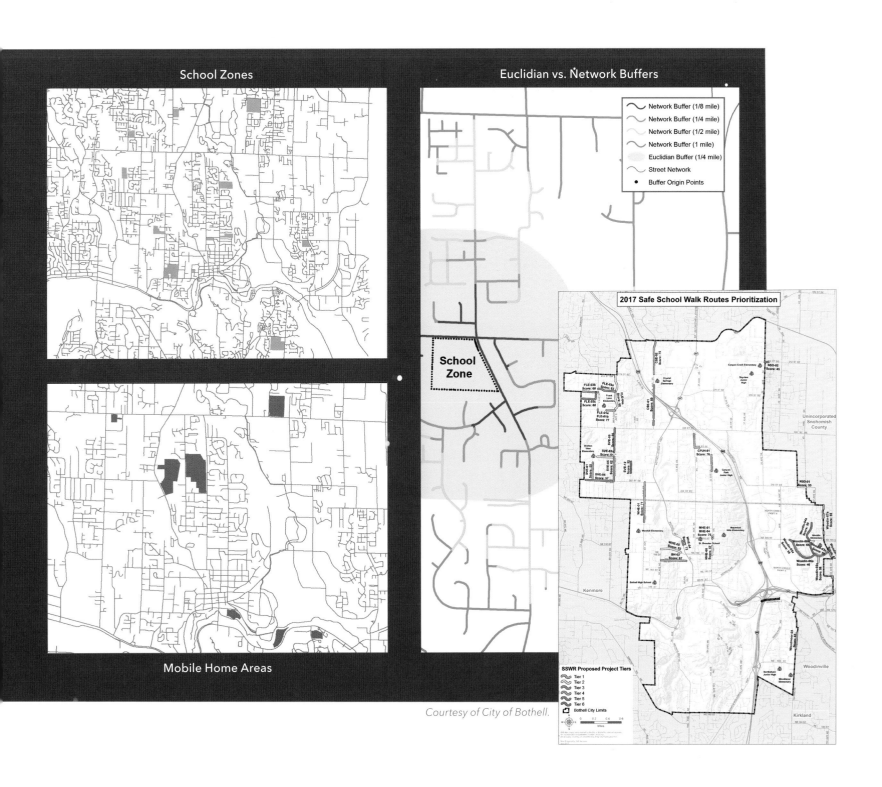

School Zones

Euclidian vs. Network Buffers

	Network Buffer (1/8 mile)
	Network Buffer (1/4 mile)
	Network Buffer (1/2 mile)
	Network Buffer (1 mile)
	Euclidian Buffer (1/4 mile)
	Street Network
●	Buffer Origin Points

School Zone

2017 Safe School Walk Routes Prioritization

SSWR Proposed Project Tiers
Tier 1
Tier 2
Tier 3
Tier 4
Tier 5
Tier 6
Bothell City Limits

Mobile Home Areas

Courtesy of City of Bothell.

the prioritization scores. The final colored prioritization spreadsheet with corresponding colored sidewalk map locations was a key tool promoting project transparency and decision-making for the advisory committee. The results of this project will help the City of Bothell plan for short-term, future, and ongoing sidewalk construction efforts.

CONTACT
Daryn Brown
daryn.brown@bothellwa.gov

SOFTWARE
ArcGIS Desktop10.3

DATA SOURCES
City of Bothell, Washington State Department of Transportation, Northshore School District

DEVELOPING A SOIL EROSION INDEX FOR THE ELK VALLEY, BRITISH COLUMBIA

British Columbia's Ministry of Forests, Lands, Natural Resources Operations, and Rural Development wanted to calculate a soil erosion index to quantify the potential impacts of road and ditch constructions to soil erosion. The study would identify high-risk areas where soil erosion can have major impacts on water quality to nearby streams and lakes. This study used publicly available soil data to provide a soil erosion index for the Elk Valley region. The study was based on soil texture, drainage, and parent material information. The erosion index was integrated to the cumulative effects research project, which aims to evaluate natural resource management impacts on ecosystems in British Columbia.

GeoBC
Victoria, British Columbia, Canada
By Steeve Deschênes and Deepa Filatow

CONTACT
Steeve Deschênes

SOFTWARE
ArcGIS Desktop 10.2

DATA SOURCE
Terrestrial Ecosystem Information dataset from the BC Ministry of Environment and Climate Change Strategy

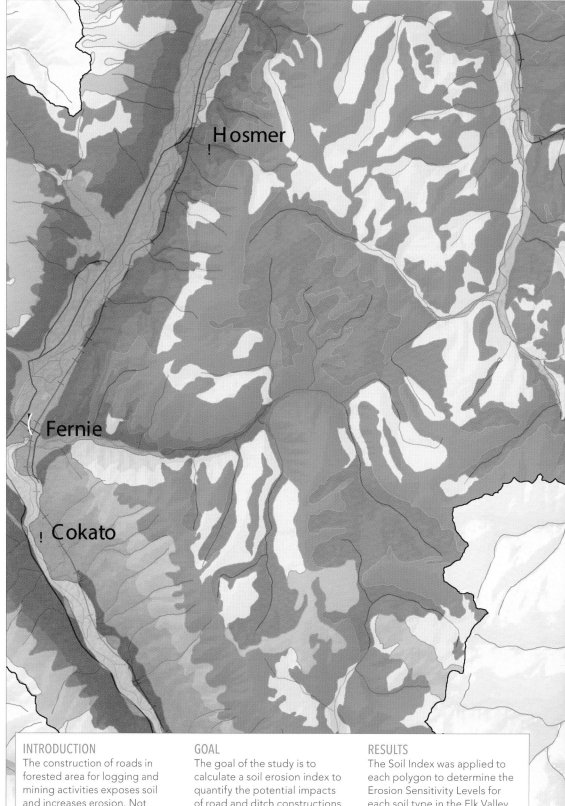

INTRODUCTION
The construction of roads in forested area for logging and mining activities exposes soil and increases erosion. Not only does the forest soil gets depleted, the sediments reach nearby streams and lakes and adversely affect the aquatic life

GOAL
The goal of the study is to calculate a soil erosion index to quantify the potential impacts of road and ditch constructions to soil erosion. The objective is to identify high risk areas where soil erosion can have major impacts on water quality to nearby streams and lakes

RESULTS
The Soil Index was applied to each polygon to determine the Erosion Sensitivity Levels for each soil type in the Elk Valley area.
Finally the Soil Erosion Index were grouped into 5 categories and colour-coded as followed (total Km2):

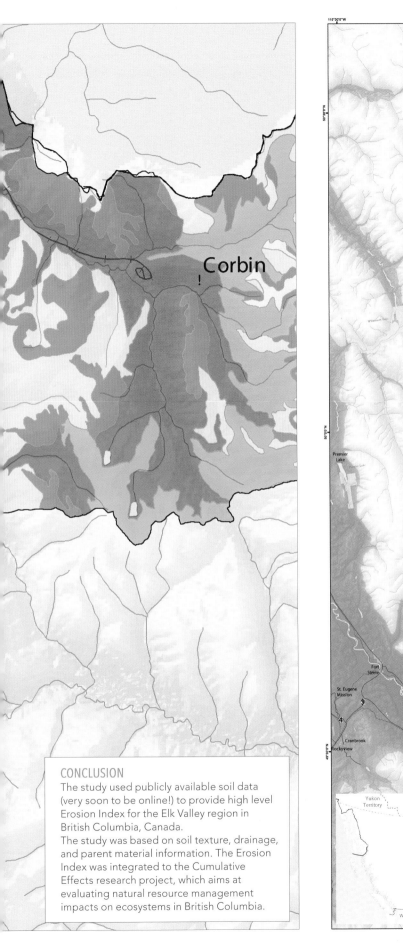

Corbin

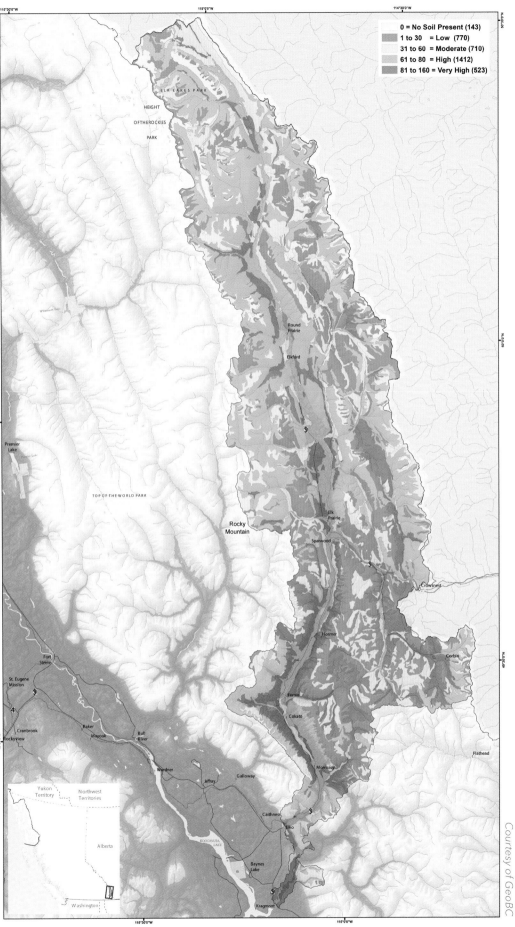

| 0 = No Soil Present (143) |
| 1 to 30 = Low (770) |
| 31 to 60 = Moderate (710) |
| 61 to 80 = High (1412) |
| 81 to 160 = Very High (523) |

CONCLUSION

The study used publicly available soil data (very soon to be online!) to provide high level Erosion Index for the Elk Valley region in British Columbia, Canada.

The study was based on soil texture, drainage, and parent material information. The Erosion Index was integrated to the Cumulative Effects research project, which aims at evaluating natural resource management impacts on ecosystems in British Columbia.

MAPPING JUNIPER ON RANGELANDS

Ashe juniper (*Juniperus ashei*) is a small, many-stemmed tree found in rocky limestone soil from central to west Texas. Also known as post cedar, mountain cedar, or blueberry juniper, the evergreen has greatly increased in abundance over the past century because of control of natural and man-caused fires and by overgrazing. Ashe juniper can be distinguished on color-infrared imagery obtained in spring and summer where it has a distinct dark reddish-brown tonal response.

This study investigated the use of the image segmentation function in ArcGIS Pro. Image segmentation creates objects where pixels having similar spectral characteristics are grouped together into a segment. Segmentation incorporates both the spectral and spatial characteristics of pixels to create image-objects defined as areas with shape and spectral homogeneity. These image objects can then be classified using traditional image classification techniques including unsupervised classification.

These maps show the results of image segmentation using imagery from the National Agriculture Imagery Program and the Sentinel-2 satellite displayed as color infrared. The NRCS plans to continue to develop these image segmentation procedures and deploy them as a tool for rapid analysis of Ashe juniper extent.

US Department of Agriculture Natural Resources Conservation Service (USDA-NRCS)
Fort Worth, Texas, USA
By Dorsey Plunk and W. Dwain Daniels

CONTACT
W. Dwain Daniels
dwain.daniels@ftw.usda.go

SOFTWARE
ArcGIS Pro 1.4

DATA SOURCES
USDA Natoinal Agriculture Imagery Program, European Space Agency Sentinel 2

Figure 1– Observations on Natural Color NAIP. Difficult to distinguish Juniper from other trees.

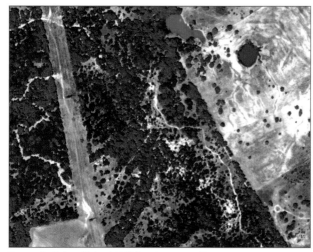

Figure 2– False Color NAIP for the area of interest. Dark-red tones are juniper trees.

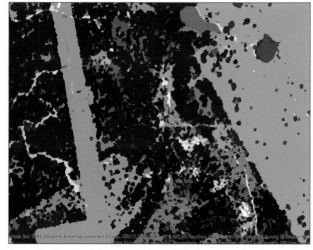

Figure 3– Result of Segment Mean Shift function. Similar pixels are grouped together.

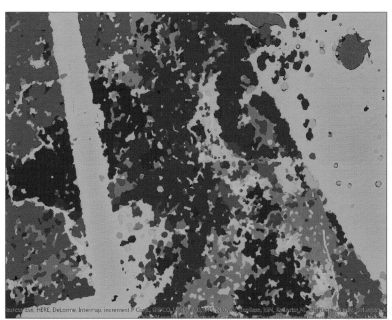

Courtesy of USDA-NRCS.

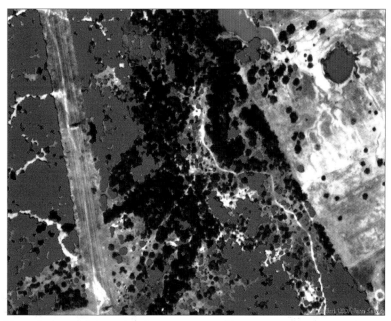

Figure 4—Results of Cluster function. Creates up to 30 groups of similar segmentation reaster pixels.

Figure 5—Result of the reclassification process. Observation points are used to ID the presence of Juniper trees in the area examined.

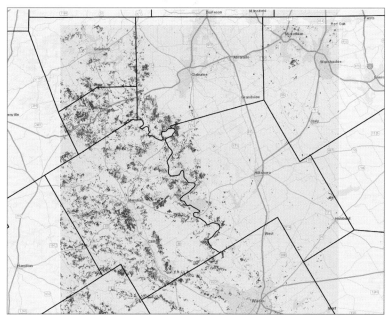

Figure 6—Process completed on European Space Agency Sentinel Imagery.

Figure 7—Using Sentinel data will result in coarser resolution, but the area of analysis can be extended to multiple counties.

Harbor Road Aerial Photo—Current Salt Marsh Extent—Rye, NH

Legend
Existing Salt Marsh
Harbor Road Outlet Watershed

0 150 300 450 600
Feet

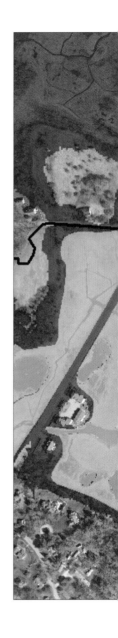

A MODERN-DAY PROTOCOL TO ASSESS TIDAL CROSSINGS

The Nature Conservancy
Concord,
New Hampshire, USA
By Shea Flanagan and
Pete Steckler

Tidal crossing infrastructure is at the front lines of coastal challenges associated with climate change, including sea level rise and more frequent and intense storm events. Climate-ready infrastructure is necessary to adapt to these challenges, allowing for the continuous flow of people, goods and services across coastal communities. Existing infrastructure may prove insufficient in its ability to handle these challenges, which poses risks to critically important and imperiled habitats and species, as well as to public safety.

The Nature Conservancy has developed a protocol to assess crossing structures that convey tidal flows within New Hampshire's Seacoast Region in partnership with the New Hampshire Department of Environmental Services' Coastal Program. This instructional map was created to illustrate the reasoning behind the development of the protocol, and to illustrate various analyses that serve as components of the protocol's assessments.

Existing Salt Marsh

2050 Salt Marsh Migration Projection
Irregularly Flooded Marsh   Regularly Flooded Marsh   Transitional Salt Marsh

0 150 300 450 600
Feet

Existing Salt Marsh

2050 1.7' Sea Level Rise with 1% Annual Flood

Salt Marsh Migration Potential–2050 1.7' Sea Level Rise

Assessment protocols to address tidal crossings are few and far between. There is an abundance of freshwater road-stream crossing protocols, but they do not address the unique and complex nature of tidal crossings. The purpose of assessing tidal crossings using this protocol is to better understand the compatibility of the crossing with the ecological system it bisects. A crossing's compatibility is assessed from the perspective of multiple management objectives, such as a structure's condition, inundation risk, and restrictiveness to tidal flows, among others. The protocol is a first screen to identify infrastructure replacement and ecological restoration priorities.

CONTACT
Shea Flanagan
shea.flanagan@tnc.org

SOFTWARE
ArcGIS Desktop 10.2

DATA SOURCES
The Nature Conservancy, New Hampshire Fish and Game Department, New Hampshire Geographically Referenced Analysis and Information Transfer System, US Fish and Wildlife Service

STRESSORS OF THE NARRAGANSETT BAY ECOSYSTEM

CSRA Inc. /US Environmental Protection Agency
Narragansett, Rhode Island, USA
By Michael Charpentier, Anne Kuhn, Eivy Monroy,
Jessica Cressman, and Juliet Swigor, Narragansett
Bay Estuary Program, University
of Rhode Island and Mass DEP

The Narragansett Bay Estuary Program developed the "State of Narragansett Bay and its Watershed" report on the ecosystem of Narragansett Bay with the support of over fifty bistate partners. The goal of the report, released in the summer of 2017, was to generate an understanding of Narragansett Bay, not as a simple body of water but as an ecosystem. The report details many environmental indicators that include stressors due to landscape, climate change, and chemicals in addition to indicators of ecosystem condition and indicators of public health.

The US Environmental Protection Agency's Atlantic Ecology Division assisted the Estuary Program with geospatial analysis and the production of maps used in the report. The maps help to convey the spatial distribution of historical population growth, the current trends of sprawl, and projections of future anthropogenic growth within the watershed. The density of onsite wastewater treatment systems (septic systems and cesspools) was estimated from low-to-high density and the population residing within the high-density areas was calculated. These maps focus on three of the landscape stressors of the Narragansett Bay ecosystem: population, land use, and the distribution of onsite wastewater systems.

CONTACT
Michael Charpentier,
charpentier.mike@epa.gov

SOFTWARE
ArcGIS Desktop 10.3

DATA SOURCES
US Census Bureau, US Geological Survey, Rhode Island Geographic Information System, Massachusetts Bureau of Geographic Information, Silvis Lab. Massachusetts Department of Environmental Protection, Rhode Island Department of Environmental Management.

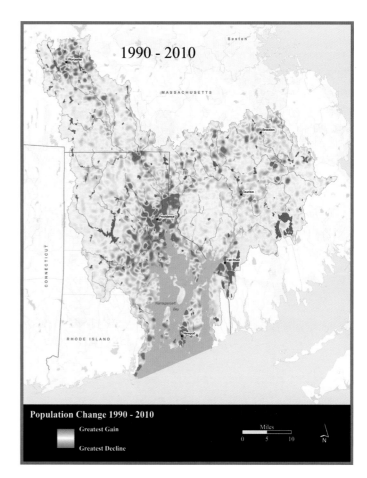

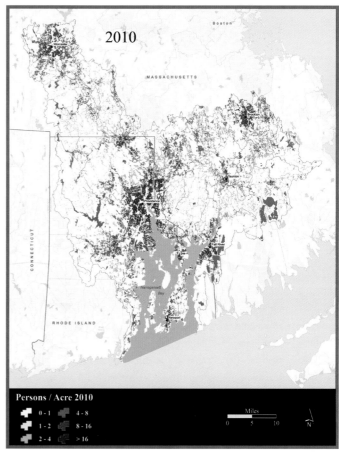

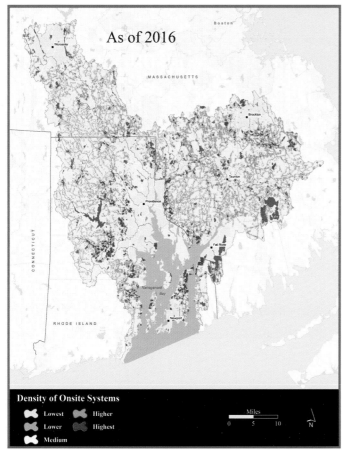

As of 2016

Density of Onsite Systems

- Lowest
- Lower
- Medium
- Higher
- Highest

Miles
0   5   10

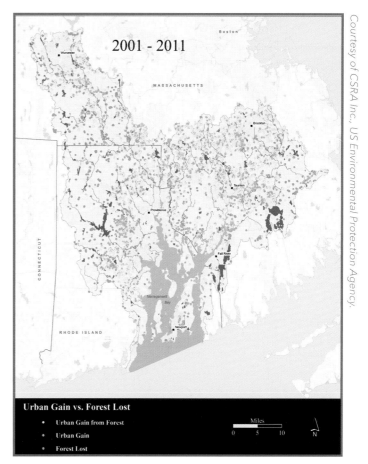

2001 - 2011

Urban Gain vs. Forest Lost

- Urban Gain from Forest
- Urban Gain
- Forest Lost

Miles
0   5   10

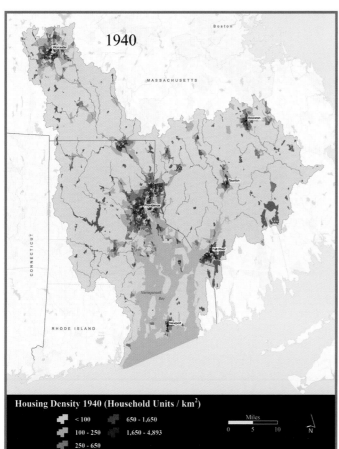

1940

Housing Density 1940 (Household Units / km²)

- < 100
- 100 - 250
- 250 - 650
- 650 - 1,650
- 1,650 - 4,893

Miles
0   5   10

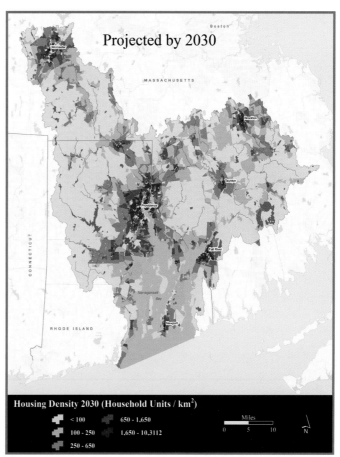

Projected by 2030

Housing Density 2030 (Household Units / km²)

- < 100
- 100 - 250
- 250 - 650
- 650 - 1,650
- 1,650 - 10,3112

Miles
0   5   10

SIMULATING THERMAL AND WIND DYNAMICS TO AID ENVIRONMENTAL PLANNING

Tokyo University of Agriculture
Setagaya, Tokyo, Japan
By Teruaki Irie

This study demonstrates how simulated thermal and wind dynamics can be integrated into urban environmental planning. Three dimensional GIS and computational fluid dynamics (CFD) simulations were employed to investigate the effects of green space and wind flows on urban cooling, using the Setagaya University campus as a case study. Researchers evaluated the current configuration of the campus in relation to its thermal environment and wind conditions and reached the following conclusions:

1) Summer daytime temperatures in a green space area for Bajikouen, an avenue of Zelkova, and a grove of Metasequoia were 2 to 3 degrees Celsius lower than urban areas within the campus.

2) Trees near the main gate help mitigate southerly wind speeds, and a campus building along Setagaya Street shelters the Bajikouen area and the Zalkova avenue from the same southerly wind.

3) Northwesterly winds are split after striking building No. 18, resulting in high winter daytime wind speeds.

4) Split wind flows from the south, striking a newly constructed research building, resulting in high summer daytime winds.

Finally, researchers evaluated proposed campus redevelopment plans based on thermal and wind dynamics, demonstrating how the simulation of the thermal environment from remotely sensed data and of wind dynamics through CFD can improve environmental planning in urban areas to the benefit of civil society.

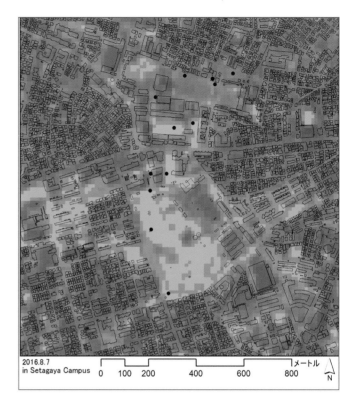

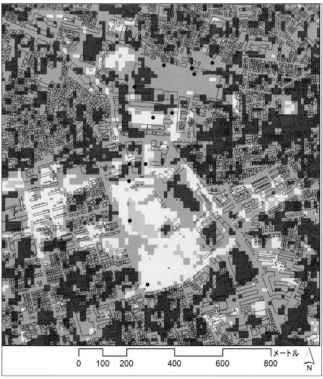

CONTACT
Teruaki Irie
teruaki0105@gmail.com

SOFTWARE
ArcGIS Desktop 10.3,
AirflowAnalyst,
ERDAS IMAGINE

DATA SOURCES
Environmental GIS Laboratory Co. for computational fluid dynamics simulations; Aster data; air temperature observation data; wind direction and speed observation data

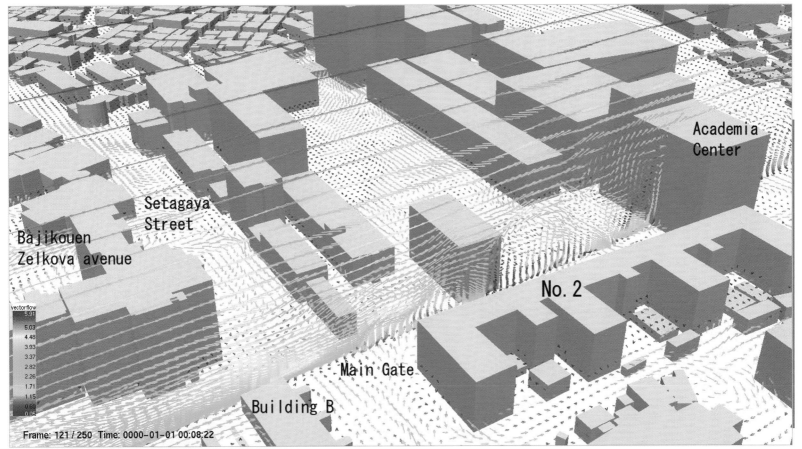

Academia
Center

Setagaya
Street

Bajikouen
Zelkova avenue

vectorflow
5.91
5.03
4.48
3.93
3.37
2.82
2.26
1.71
1.15
0.60
0.05

No. 2

Main Gate

Building B

Frame: 121 / 250 Time: 0000-01-01 00:08:22

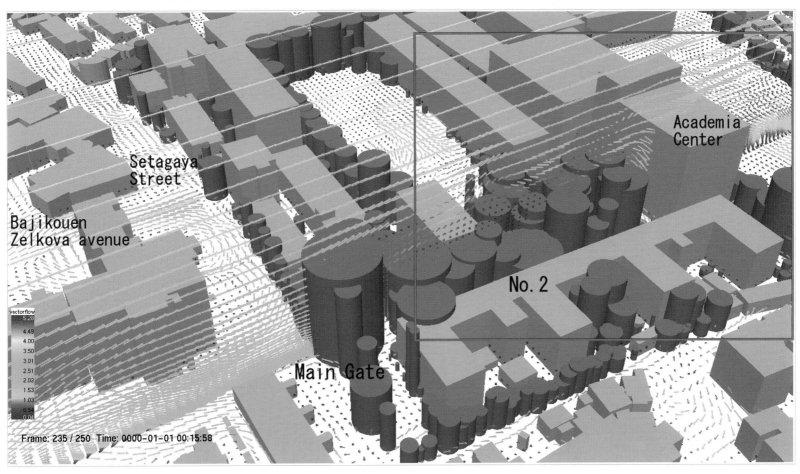

Setagaya
Street

Bajikouen
Zelkova avenue

Academia
Center

No. 2

vectorflow
5.28
4.49
4.00
3.50
3.01
2.51
2.02
1.53
1.03
0.54
0.04

Main Gate

Frame: 235 / 250 Time: 0000-01-01 00:15:58

WATERSHED ECOSYSTEM SERVICES TOOL (WESTOOL)

Blue Raster, LLC
Arlington, Virginia, USA
By Blue Raster, LLC / Winrock International

WESTool Water Analysis

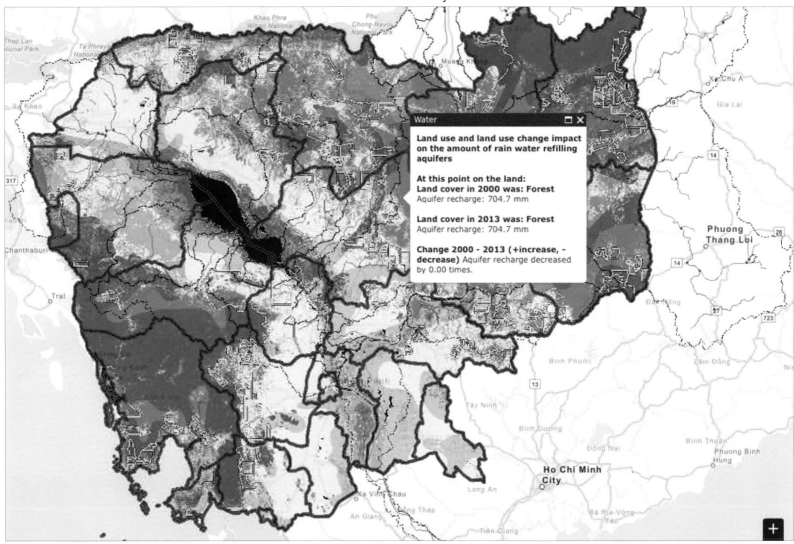

Water

Land use and land use change impact on the amount of rain water refilling aquifers

At this point on the land:
Land cover in 2000 was: Forest
Aquifer recharge: 704.7 mm

Land cover in 2013 was: Forest
Aquifer recharge: 704.7 mm

Change 2000 - 2013 (+increase, - decrease) Aquifer recharge decreased by 0.00 times.

Blue Raster, Winrock International, and the US Agency for International Development (USAID) partnered to produce the Watershed Ecosystem Services Tool (WESTool). This innovative application allows users to explore the interaction of ecosystem services, land uses, and socioeconomic factors across Cambodia's landscapes. By combining advanced science with intuitive maps and tools, the WESTool offers valuable information at the local, regional, and national scale to support decision-makers and land-managers who wish to understand and balance the value of remaining forests with development goals.

The WESTool estimates land-use change, carbon stocks, greenhouse gas emissions, sediment and nutrient loss, changes in river water quality, impacts on biodiversity, population, access to market, and general agricultural production data at the national and local levels in Cambodia. This provides a valuable resource for anyone interested in learning more about the impacts of

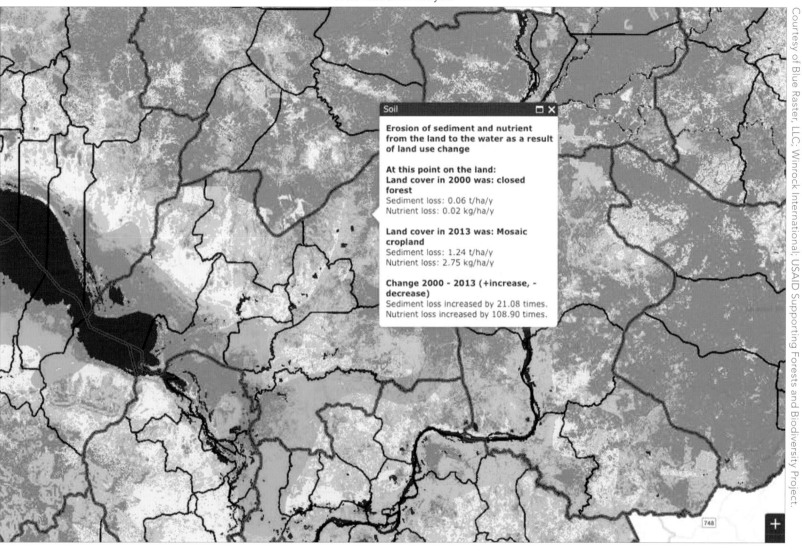

land-use change on forest ecosystem services, people, and the economy in Cambodia. The tool provides for a more comprehensive understanding of the implications of land-management decisions by offering information on both the historical impacts of land-use change and the current value of ecosystem services.

CONTACT
Michael Lippmann
mlippmann@blueraster.com

SOFTWARE
ArcGIS Server, ArcGIS Online, ArcGIS Desktop 10.4

DATA SOURCE
Winrock International

ABU DHABI DOCUMENTED COASTAL AND MARINE HABITATS AND SPECIES

This map represents the documented habitats of importance and species as identified by the Environment Agency—Abu Dhabi (EAD) within the coastal and marine area of the Emirate of Abu Dhabi. Moreover, it illustrates other uses and activities affecting these natural resources such as existing and proposed Marine Protected Areas, fishing grounds, dredged areas, important bird areas, and important turtle areas.

EAD is a governmental agency that was established in 1996 and is committed to protecting and managing biodiversity, providing a clean environment, and promoting sustainable development in Abu Dhabi.

Abu Dhabi Urban Planning Council
Abu Dhabi, United Arab Emirates
By Abu Dhabi Urban Planning Council

CONTACT
Samer Atiya
satiya@gmail.com

SOFTWARE
ArcGIS Desktop

DATA SOURCE
Abu Dhabi Urban Planning Council

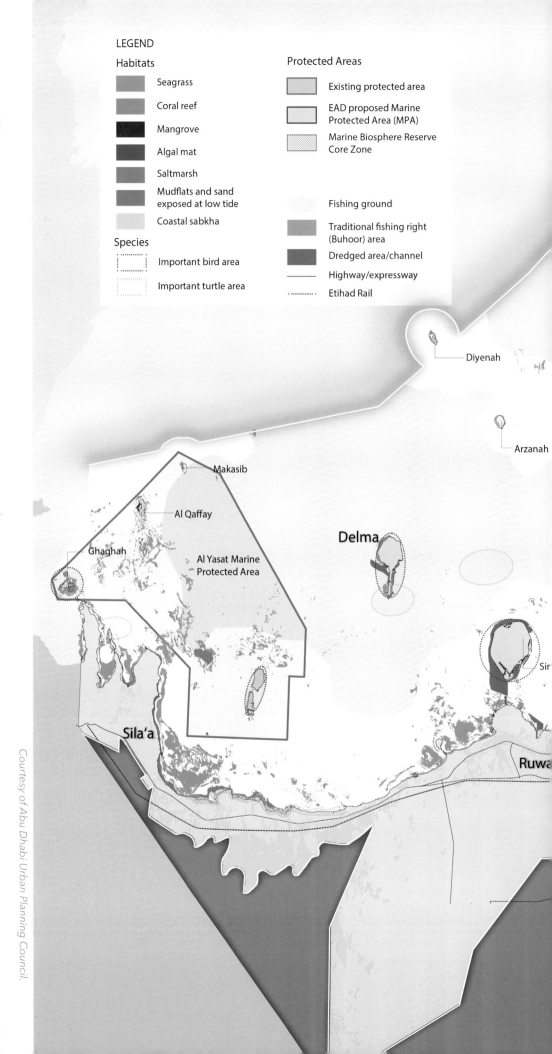

LEGEND

Habitats

Seagrass
Coral reef
Mangrove
Algal mat
Saltmarsh
Mudflats and sand exposed at low tide
Coastal sabkha

Species

Important bird area
Important turtle area

Protected Areas

Existing protected area
EAD proposed Marine Protected Area (MPA)
Marine Biosphere Reserve Core Zone

Fishing ground
Traditional fishing right (Buhoor) area
Dredged area/channel
Highway/expressway
Etihad Rail

Diyenah
Arzanah
Makasib
Al Qaffay
Delma
Ghaghah
Al Yasat Marine Protected Area
Sir
Sila'a
Ruwa

Courtesy of Abu Dhabi Urban Planning Council.

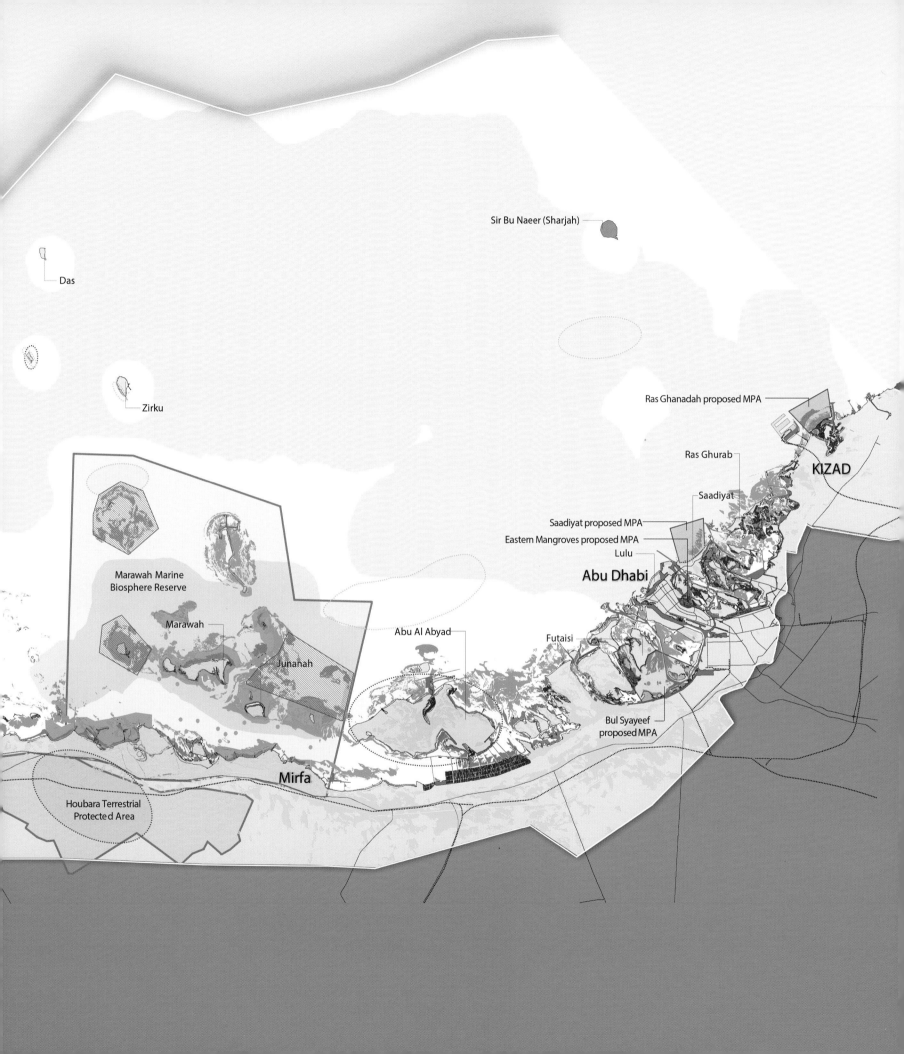

Sir Bu Naeer (Sharjah)

Das

Zirku

Ras Ghanadah proposed MPA

KIZAD

Ras Ghurab

Saadiyat

Saadiyat proposed MPA

Eastern Mangroves proposed MPA

Lulu

Marawah Marine
Biosphere Reserve

Abu Dhabi

Marawah

Abu Al Abyad

Junanah

Futaisi

Mirfa

Bul Syayeef
proposed MPA

Houbara Terrestrial
Protected Area

MARITIME 2030 EMIRATE-WIDE FRAMEWORK PLAN

Maritime, coastal, and marine areas through a stringent process of review and analysis into a single spatial plan. Its goals include balancing economic growth and societal needs, quality of life with marine conservation, and providing efficient and environmentally aware maritime transport solutions.

Based on the ten challenges that have been identified in Plan Maritime 2030, this overall emirate-wide framework plan map illustrates a balanced approach to allocating multiple future uses and activities within the coastal and marine area of Abu Dhabi that will help shape the future development of a safe, secure, and sustainable maritime domain.

Abu Dhabi Urban Planning Council
Abu Dhabi, United Arab Emirates
By Abu Dhabi Urban Planning Council

CONTACT
Samer Atiya
satiya@gmail.com

SOFTWARE
ArcGIS Desktop

DATA SOURCE
Abu Dhabi Urban Planning Council

Courtesy of Abu Dhabi Urban Planning Council.

Transboundary
ecological
connection

Sir Bu Naeer
(Sharjah)

Zirku

Khalifa Port

KIZAD

Ras Ghurab

Saadiyat

Marawah Marine
Biosphere Reserve

Lulu

Abu Dhabi

Marawah

Abu Al Abyad

Futaisi

Junanah

Mirfa

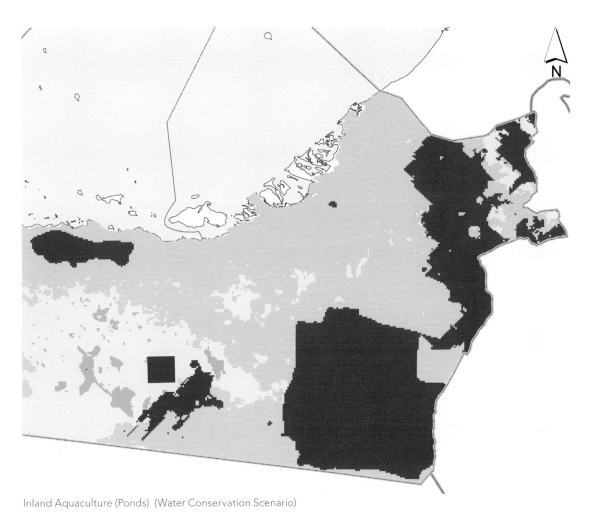

Inland Aquaculture (Ponds) (Water Conservation Scenario)

Seacages Aquaculture Suitability

AQUACULTURE IN ABU DHABI

Environmental Agency
Abu Dhabi
Abu Dhabi, United Arab
Emirates
By Environmental
Agency Abu Dhabi

The aquaculture industry is growing rapidly in the Emirate of Abu Dhabi due to the increase in population, increased nutritional demand, and associated over-exploitation of the local fish stock. The industry provides an alternative protein source and could provide opportunities for economic growth and entrepreneurship among the local community. It is against this backdrop that Environmental Agency Abu Dhabi performed an analysis to select and prioritize

areas suitable for aquaculture along the coast as well as inland areas.

This selection approach involved analysis for three different types of aquaculture: inland aquaculture systems, sea cages, and intertidal aquaculture. Accordingly, there were three distinct analysis domains defined to enable the process of site selection leading to three sets of suitability predictors and classifications.

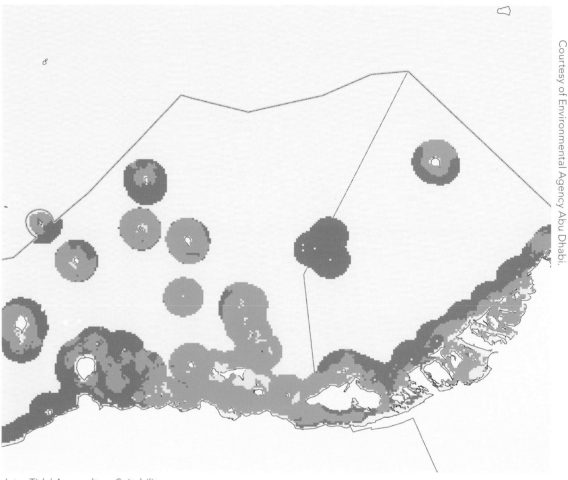

Inter-Tidal Aquaculture Suitability

Courtesy of Environmental Agency Abu Dhabi.

For example, the distance to critical marine habitats such as mangroves, sea grass, and coral reefs were considered when processing for coastal aquaculture, while these had no value when modeling for inland aquaculture suitability. The approach resulted in three sets of prioritized areas to be used for purposes of the specified aquaculture activity.

CONTACT
Samer Atiya
satiya@gmail.com

SOFTWARE
ArcGIS Desktop

DATA SOURCE
Environmental Agency
Abu Dhabi

LIGHT POLLUTION IN THE UNITED KINGDOM

Stars are a source of infinite amazement for scientists, casual observers, and millions seeking rural places to rest and recuperate, but the view is obscured by light pollution. Many children will grow up never seeing the Milky Way, our own galaxy, because of the impact of artificial light.

This map used satellite data to create the most detailed maps ever of Britain's light pollution and dark skies, allowing free public access to information identifying where light is spilling up into the night sky and where urgent action is needed. GIS spatial analysis was used to process and classify the satellite data into bands to support meaningful quantitative analysis. Spatial statistics tools were used to analyze and present the data, identifying patterns and reporting the findings in a clear way.

LUC
Bristol, United Kingdom
By Diana Manson and Chris Green

CONTACT
Diana Manson
diana.manson@landuse.co.uk

SOFTWARE
ArcGIS Desktop 10.4.1

DATA SOURCES
Earth Observation Group, National Oceanic and Atmospheric Administration's National Centers for Environmental Information, OpenStreetMap contributors

Courtesy of LUC and Campaign to Protect Rural England.

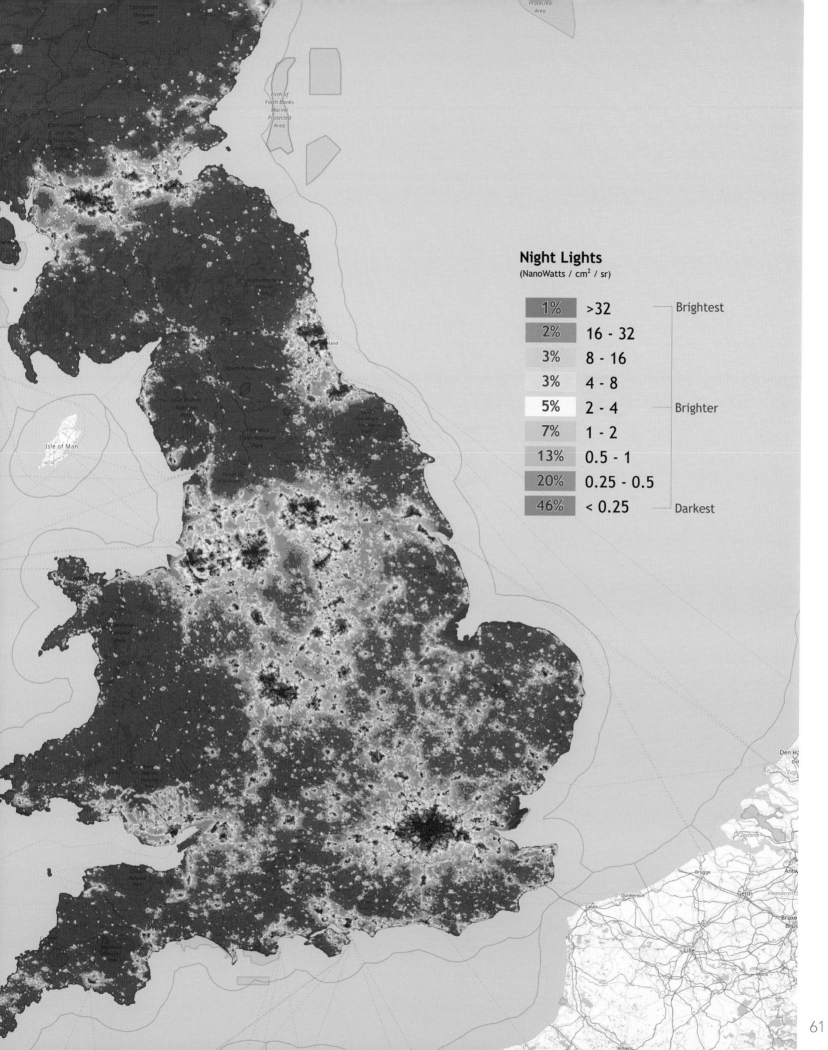

Night Lights

(NanoWatts / cm² / sr)

1%	>32	Brightest
2%	16 - 32	
3%	8 - 16	
3%	4 - 8	
5%	2 - 4	Brighter
7%	1 - 2	
13%	0.5 - 1	
20%	0.25 - 0.5	
46%	< 0.25	Darkest

FORECASTING OF OIL SPILL FOR THE UNDERWATER PIPELINE

This map shows a hypothetical situation of damage to the underwater pipeline in the Belaya River in Russia. The map, created with hydrodynamic modeling, can be used for making decisions about the placement of emergency responders. Shown here are a depth map and a velocity map and point to the time of an arriving oil spot.

IntroGIS
Ufa, Republic of Bashkortostan, Russia
By Sergei Mitakovich

CONTACT
Sergei Mitakovich
S.Mitakovich@introgis.ru

SOFTWARE
ArcGIS Desktop

DATA SOURCES
Common topographic maps, processed pilotage maps

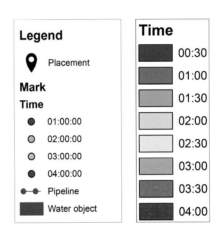

Depth

ЕЭКО © Росреестр 2010

Velocity

ЕЭКО © Росреестр 2010

CRIME PREDICTION IN GREATER LONDON USING MACHINE LEARNING

In this interactive map, the user can change layers for viewing Greater London crime predictions in 2017, crime-type patterns from previous years, and other metrics based on Machine Learning algorithms from Dataiku Data Science Studio. Different predictive models have been built depending on the required level of prediction and variables from prepared raw data.

Thanks to data provided by data.police.uk, the site for open data about crime and policing in England, Wales, and Northern Ireland, users can focus on specific Lower Super Output Areas to anticipate the number of crimes and their types. A month-by-month check on published data demonstrates the forecasts' stability and fit to reality. The redder the area, the larger the number of crimes predicted.

DATAIKU
New York, New York, USA
By Nicholas Gakrelidz

CONTACT
By Nicolas Gakrelidz
nicolas.gakrelidz@dataiku.com

SOFTWARE
ArcGIS Online

DATA SOURCE
Data Police UK (https://data.police.uk/data/)

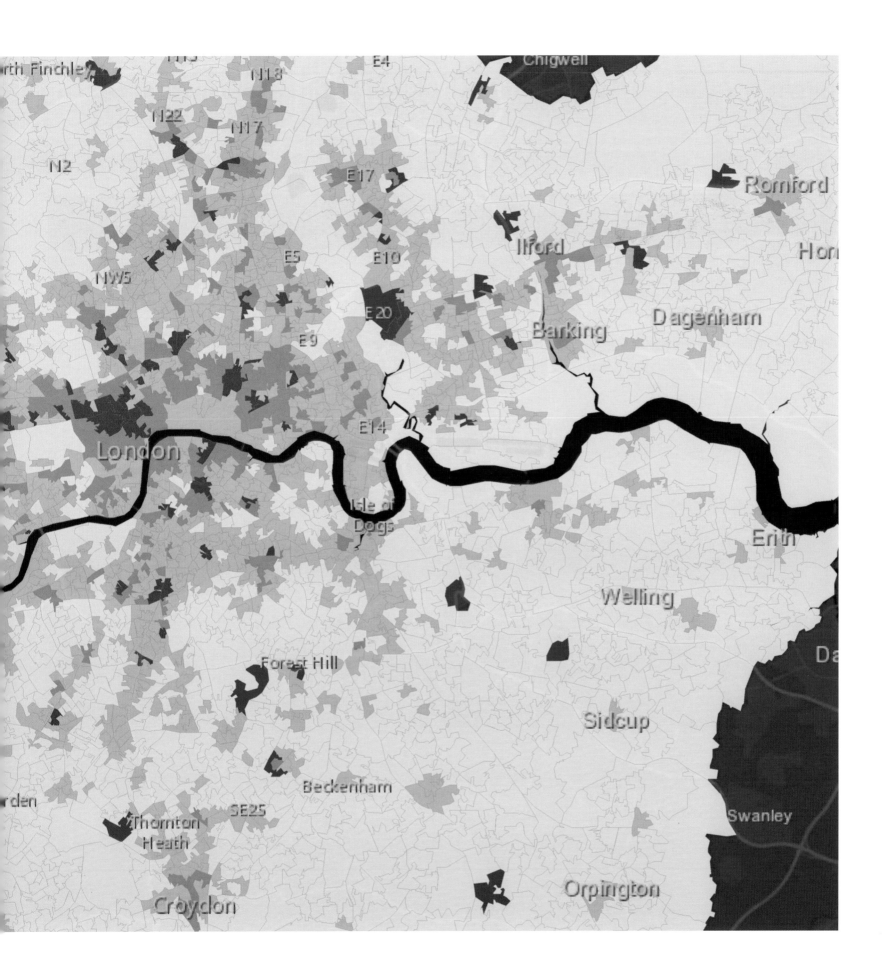

CREATING A SAFETY MAP TO REDUCE CRIME AND TRAFFIC ACCIDENTS

Aichi Prefectural Police Headquarters
Nagoya, Aichi, Japan
By Department of Community Safety, Aichi Prefectural Police

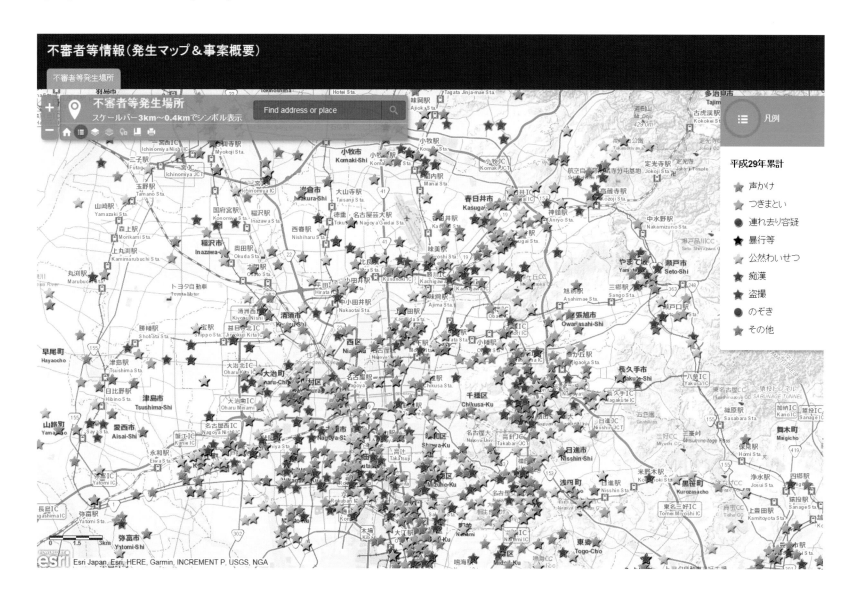

Aichi Prefecture is the focus of the Chukyo Metropolitan Area, the third-most populous metropolitan area in Japan. The greater the population, the greater the number of offenders. Aichi Prefectural Police is working to prevent crime and establish an Aichi where residents can live safely.

In 2016, Aichi Prefectural Police released an ArcGIS Online-based safety map that provides residents with information about crimes and traffic accidents. The safety map consists of the following:

- Crime information (a distribution map of seven major crimes including burglary and theft).

- Suspicious person information (a distribution map of reported child accosting and other bad acts).

- Traffic accident information (a distribution map of accidents with fatalities or serious injuries).

The safety maps also offer graphs of when crimes and accidents occurred that residents can easily understand. By informing the public when, where, and what kind of crime/traffic accident is happening, it is expected to increase awareness of safety in the area and lead to crime and accident prevention.

CONTACT
Esri Japan
gisinfo@esrij.com

SOFTWARE
ArcGIS Desktop
ArcGIS® Tracking Analyst,
ArcGIS Geosuite,
ArcGIS® Network Analyst,
ArcGIS Online, ArcGIS
Desktop, ArcGIS® Spatial
Analyst

DATA SOURCE
Aichi Prefectural Police

USING MODELBUILDER TO CREATE HURRICANE STORM SURGE ZONES

The Hurricane Storm Surge Tools are a series of models that have been created within ArcGIS Pro's ModelBuilder to automate the process of creating hurricane storm surge maps. The Sea, Lake and Overland Surges from Hurricanes (SLOSH) is a computerized numerical model developed by the National Weather Service to estimate storm surge heights resulting from historical, hypothetical, or predicted hurricanes by considering the atmospheric pressure, size, forward speed, and track data.

The difference between the surge heights calculated by the SLOSH model for each category of hurricane and the ground heights from a digital elevation model are used to determine the extents of the potential storm surge seen on the map.

US Army Corps of Engineers (USACE)
Baltimore, Maryland, USA
By Jared Scott

CONTACT
Jared Scott
jared.m.scott@usace.army.mil

SOFTWARE
ArcGIS Pro 1.4

DATA SOURCES
City of Baltimore's Open Data Catalog, Maryland iMAP, Johnson Space Center's Earth Sciences & Image Analysis Laboratory

Gridded storm surge output for Baltimore

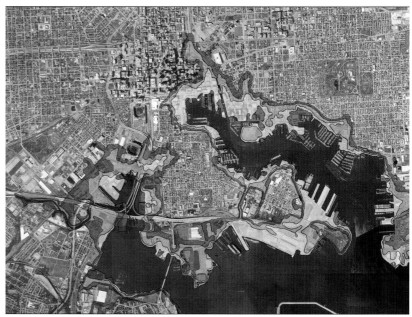

Polygon storm surge output for Baltimore

Building color indicates minimum category hurricane
that could potentially result in storm surge impact.

Potential Hurricane Storm Surge at the Inner Harbor in Baltimore

represents 50 buildings

5% annual chance of flooding

1% annu

ENCROACHING FLOOD WATERS

JBA Risk Management
Skipton, North Yorkshire,
United Kingdom
By Jessica Boyd

The city of Carlisle in Cumbria County, England, is no stranger to flooding. Flood events have been recorded in Carlisle as far back as the 1700s. More recently, significant floods have occurred in 1963, 1968, 1979, 1980, 1984, 2005, 2009, and 2015, affecting thousands of homes and businesses and causing massive insured and economic losses.

Flood hazard maps identify the locations of potential

future inundation. Some of these areas may not have been flooded in living memory, even in frequently flooded places such as Carlisle. As the severity of flooding increases, the annual chance of occurrence decreases, such that a flood with a lower chance of occurrence will have a more severe and widespread effect on people and property.

Identifying properties that may be affected by severe

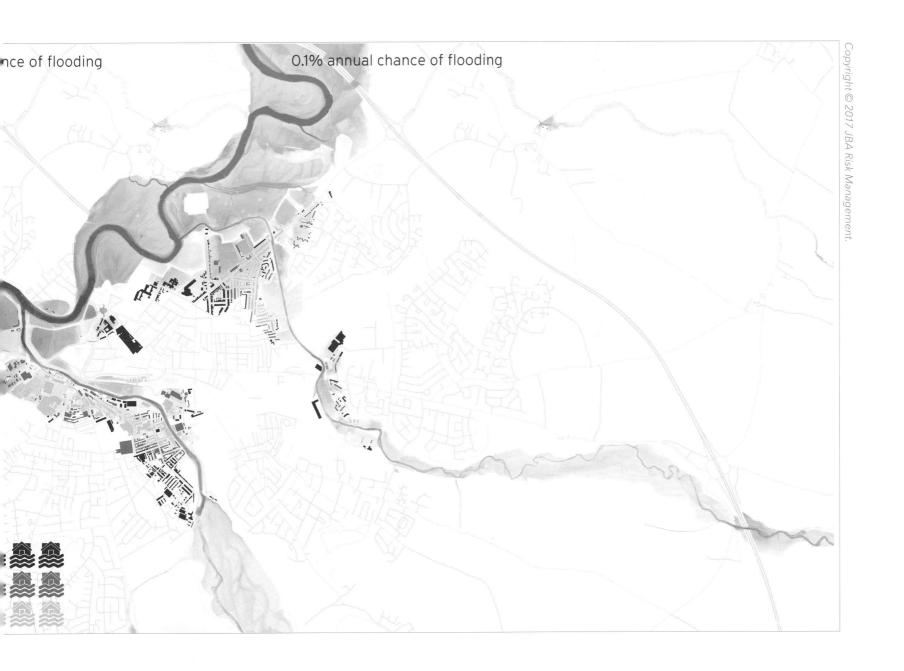

ce of flooding

0.1% annual chance of flooding

(and rare) flood events is key for reducing the impact the flood may have. If properties are identified as at-risk to flooding, resistance and resilience measures can be implemented long before the first raindrops start to fall. The level of preparedness often corresponds to the annual chance of flooding; properties with a relatively high chance of flooding annual probability often invest more in flood protection than those with a relatively low chance of flooding.

CONTACT
Jessica Boyd
jessica.boyd@jbarisk.com

SOFTWARE
ArcGIS Desktop 10.4.1

DATA SOURCES
JBA Risk Management,
Ordnance Survey

GLOBAL RIVER FLOOD MAPPING

JBA Risk Management
Skipton, North Yorkshire,
United Kingdom
By Philip Oldham

Flooding is a global problem, and increasing flood frequency brings into sharp focus the need for high-resolution hazard maps to aid with managing the risk posed by severe flooding. Hazard maps give the user information about the extent and depth of flood waters as well as the likelihood that those depths will be experienced. Using this information can aid planners, insurers, disaster risk specialists, humanitarian organizations, and others in making decisions about how best to manage the flood risk posed in a particular area.

To this end, JBA Risk Management has produced the world's first consistent global flood map that enables

Wuhan
Daji
Zhifang
Jinkou
Miaoshan

Baniyatar
BASUNDH
GONGABU
SUKED
BANASTHALI BALUWATAR
THAMEL
CHABAHII
Kankali
GANESH
MANDIR
Maitri Nagar
NEW
BANESHWOR
SANEPA
CHOWK
gaun   Kirtipur   Patan
CHOBHAR
CHOBHAR
Phool Bari
Chowk
Taudaha

detailed investigation of flood risk at any location on the planet. Sophisticated modelling techniques and high-resolution terrain data helped create a unique dataset that is used by governments, insurance companies, and other financial institutions.

CONTACT
Philip Oldham
philip.oldham@jbarisk.com

SOFTWARE
ArcGIS Desktop 10.4.1,
Adobe Photoshop CS5

DATA SOURCE
JBA Risk Management

TACKLETOX.COM— A NEW WAY TO CHECK TOXIC CHEMICALS

Tackletox.com provides information on toxic chemicals emitted by corporations around the world. Some chemical substances are too complicated to distinguish and pronounce. Which chemical substance contains cancer-causing agent? How much chemical substances have been emitted by companies? How hazardous are they to neighborhood, animals, plants and our health? Mapping, clustering, and layering the toxicity of the area using ArcGIS can show and explain to users how safe their areas are.

Who's GOOD Korea
Seoul, Yeongdeungpo-gu,
Republic of Korea
By Sarah Lee

CONTACT
Sarah Lee
minyelee@whosgood.org

SOFTWARE
ArcGIS® API 3.20 for JavaScript™

DATA SOURCES
US Environmental Protection Agency,
Korean Pollutant Release and Transfer
Register (K-PRTR)

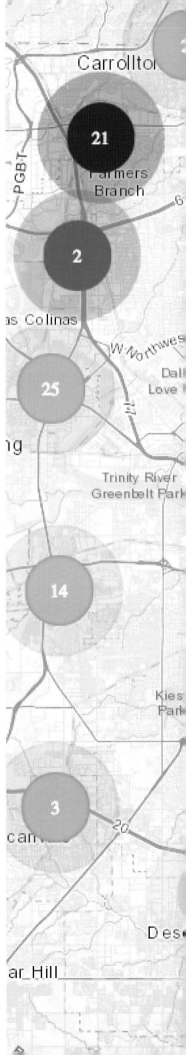

Courtesy of Who'sGOOD Korea.

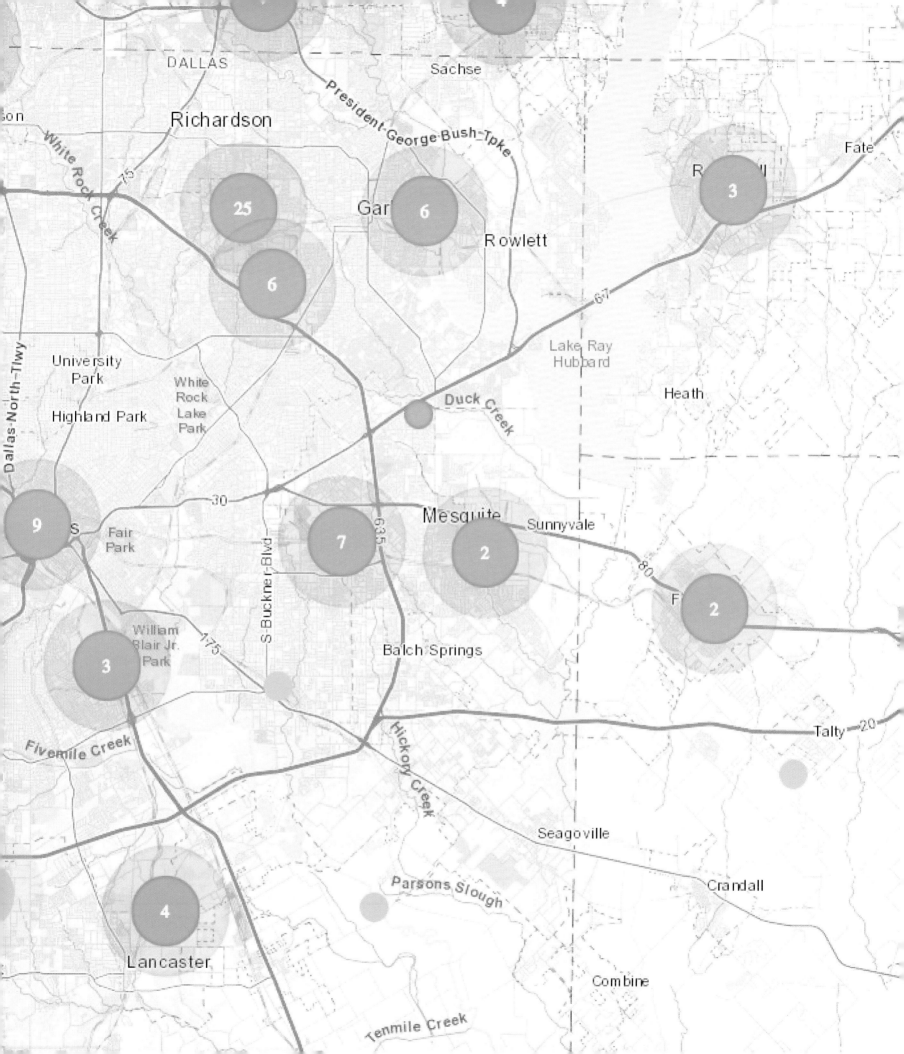

NEW YORK GEOGRAPHIC INFORMATION GATEWAY

Risk assessment helps communities understand, identify, and delineate key areas vulnerable to future storms and flooding. While several products exist to help people identify flood risk, no single product characterizes the cumulative flood risks facing coastal communities. The New York Department of State partnered with the National Oceanic and Atmospheric Administration and the Federal Emergency Management Agency to combine different pieces of information to identify New York's most vulnerable coastal areas. The result was the "DOS Coastal Risk Areas" which classify areas of extreme, high, and moderate risk for use in future resilience planning.

Stone Environmental
Montpelier, Vermont, USA
By Jeff Herter, Katie Budreski, Rebecca Newell, Peter Lauridsen, Alex Kuttesch, Alan Hammersmith, and Nick Floersch

CONTACT
Jeff Herter
Jeff.Herter@dos.ny.gov

SOFTWARE
ArcGIS Server

DATA SOURCES
New York Department of State's Office of Planning and Development, Esri

Courtesy of New York Office of Planning and Development and Stone Environmental.

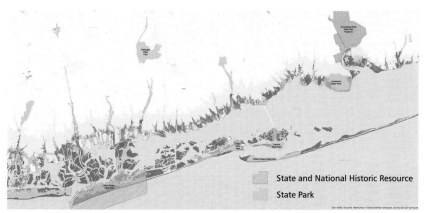

DOS Risk Areas in Action: State OPRHP and SHPO Vulnerability Assessments

State and National Historic Resource

State Park

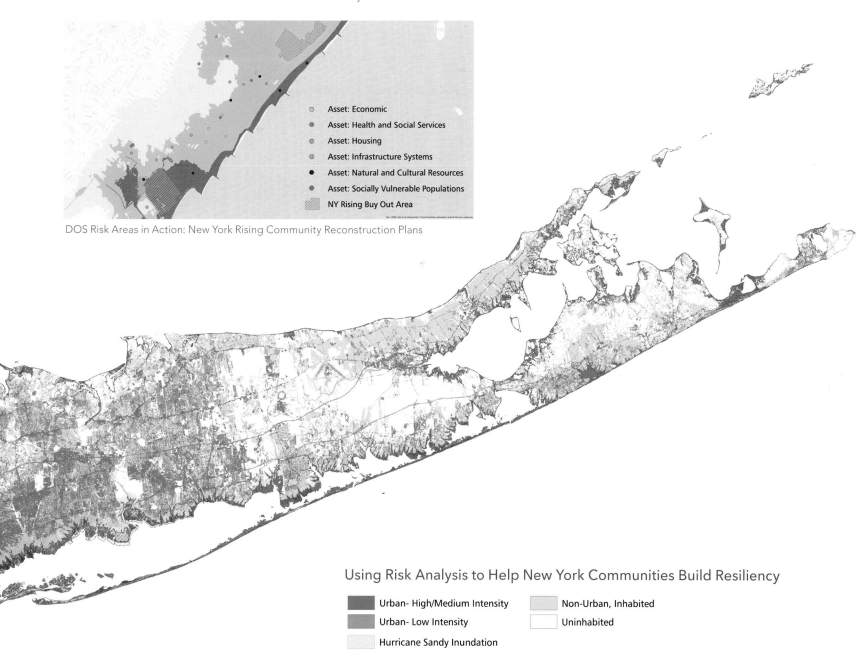

DOS Risk Areas in Action: New York Rising Community Reconstruction Plans

○ Asset: Economic

● Asset: Health and Social Services

○ Asset: Housing

○ Asset: Infrastructure Systems

● Asset: Natural and Cultural Resources

● Asset: Socially Vulnerable Populations

▨ NY Rising Buy Out Area

Using Risk Analysis to Help New York Communities Build Resiliency

Urban- High/Medium Intensity

Urban- Low Intensity

Hurricane Sandy Inundation

Non-Urban, Inhabited

Uninhabited

THE GREAT FLOOD OF 2016

City of Baton Rouge/ Parish of East Baton Rouge
Baton Rouge, Louisiana, USA
By Brandon Jumonville, Justin Priola, GISP; and Warren Kron, GISP

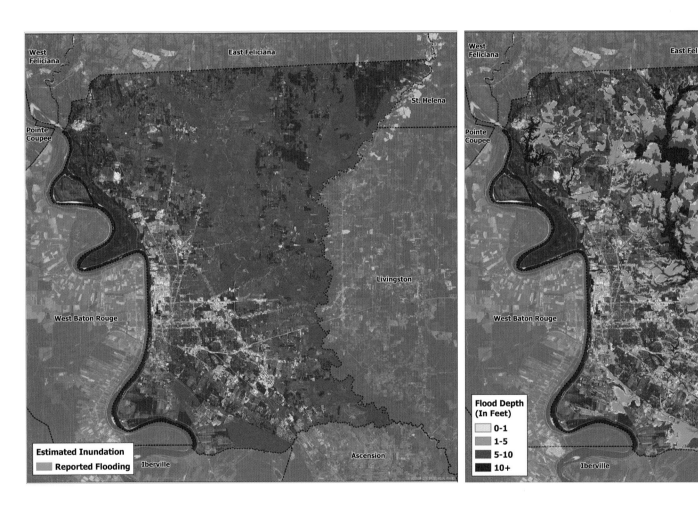

These maps display the outcome of a variety of data development, analysis, and validation techniques that provide an overview of the Great Flood of 2016 and its impact on the City of Baton Rouge and East Baton Rouge Parish, Louisiana.

One map displays the results of an innovative approach to quickly and accurately estimate the inundation area. This layer was created by aggregating numerous types of data points based on 911 calls, 311 calls, search and rescue callouts, etc., with census blocks and flood hazard areas. Additionally, the layer was made public to solicit citizen feedback to improve the accuracy of the inundation layer.

Another map displays a similar inundation layer, but one that was created with completely different data and processes. This map portrays the flood depth and was generated using high water survey marks, a digital elevation model, and watershed boundaries. Notice the overall similarity between the total inundated area as displayed in these two maps.

The other two maps display flood debris collection hotspots and streets that were under more than one foot of floodwater. Again, the data and processes used to create these two maps were totally different, but the results validate each other. Logically, more debris would be picked up in areas where the streets were flooded by more than one foot of stormwater, and this is evidenced by comparing the debris hotspots with the flooded streets.

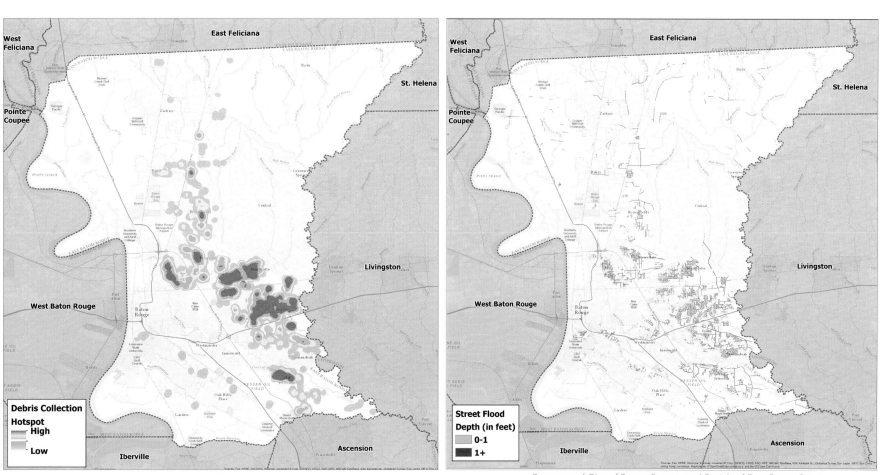

Courtesy of City of Baton Rouge and Parish of East Baton Rouge.

CONTACT
Warren Kron
wkron@brgov.com

SOFTWARE
ArcGIS Desktop 10.4.1,
ArcGIS Pro 1.4.1

DATA SOURCES
City of Baton Rouge and Parish of East Baton Rouge, US Geological
Survey, Amite River Basin Commission, Federal Emergency
Management Agency, US Census Bureau, National Oceanic and
Atmospheric Administration, Civil Air Patrol

URBAN CLIMATE VULNERABILITY MAP

This map analyzes the areas vulnerable to flooding in Seoul city using the MaxEnt model. MaxEnt is a multipurpose mechanical learning model developed from statistical mechanics and the information theory principle, which explains the probability distribution of having maximum entropy.

A model was mapped out by selecting flood-inducing factors and applying establishing data to the model. Evaluation variables were divided into physical environment, climate environment, green space environment, and artificial environment and how results change by adding variable features. The maps shown here include flood inundation in Seoul, the ratio of the flood prediction area against the drainage basin area, and the ratio of the flood protection area against the built-up area.

Korea Institute of Civil Engineering and Building Technology
Goyang-si, Republic of Korea
By Hyomin Kim

CONTACT
Hyomin Kim
hyominkim@kict.re.kr

SOFTWARE
ArcGIS Desktop 10.1

DATA SOURCE
Seoul city data

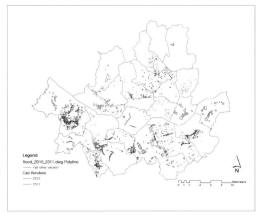

Flood inundation map in Seoul city

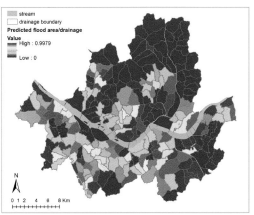

The ratio of flood prediction area against drainage basin area

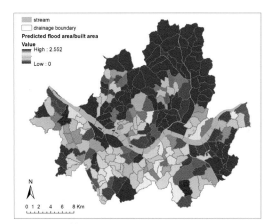

The radio of flood predication area against built-up area

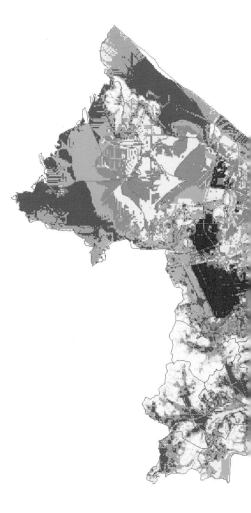

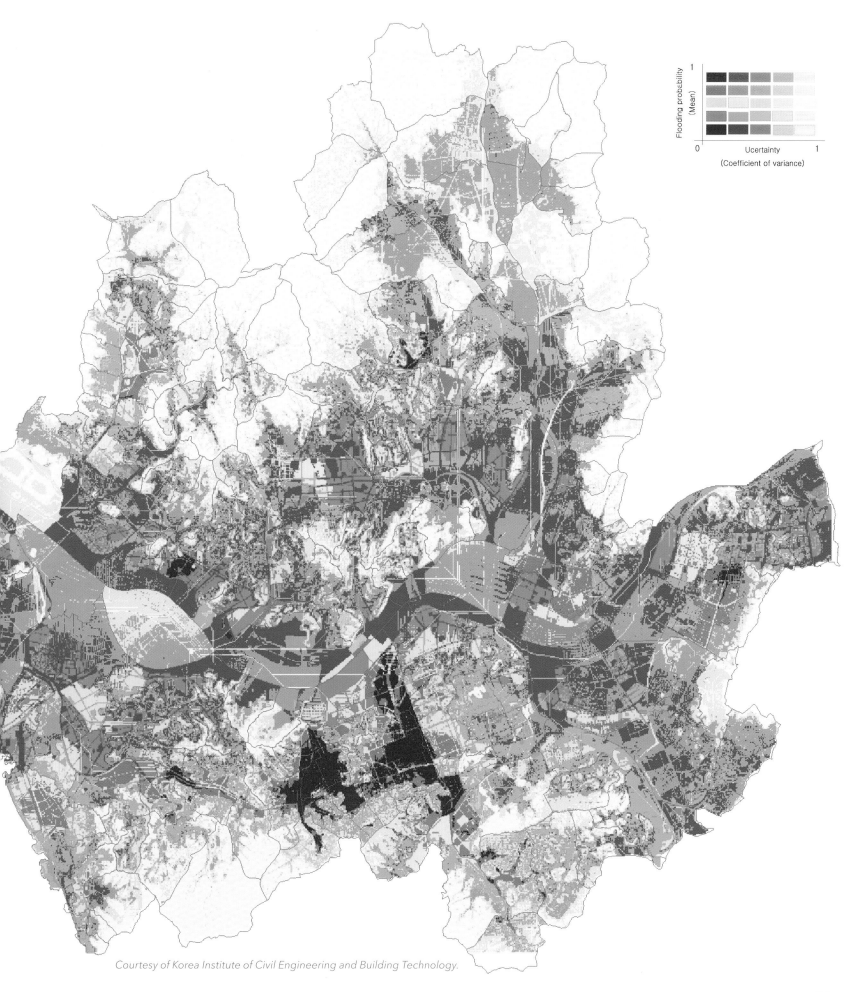

Flooding probebility
(Mean)

Ucertainty
(Coefficient of variance)

Courtesy of Korea Institute of Civil Engineering and Building Technology.

81

A COASTAL RESILIENCY ASSESSMENT FOR THE US EAST COAST

University of North Carolina Asheville, National Environmental Modeling and Analysis Center (NEMAC)
Ashville, North Carolina, USA
By Ian Johnson, Kim Rhodes, and Greg Dobson (NEMAC), and Mandy Chesnut (National Fish and Wildlife Foundation).

To assist the National Fish and Wildlife Foundation's grant funding of fish and wildlife restoration projects following major coastal storm events, NEMAC developed a GIS-based coastal resiliency assessment to give staff a decision-making tool for understanding where restoration projects could benefit fish and wildlife habitats while also increasing the resiliency of coastal communities.

The assessment process identifies landscapes where community and natural assets are potentially exposed to coastal hazards. Through the integration of GIS-based analyses with a vulnerability assessment methodology and using raster modeling and spatial analysis techniques, two key composite index layers were created to 1) inform areas of high threats by compiling coastal flood-related datasets and 2) to highlight areas of dense critical community assets by integrating a plethora of infrastructure and population datasets.

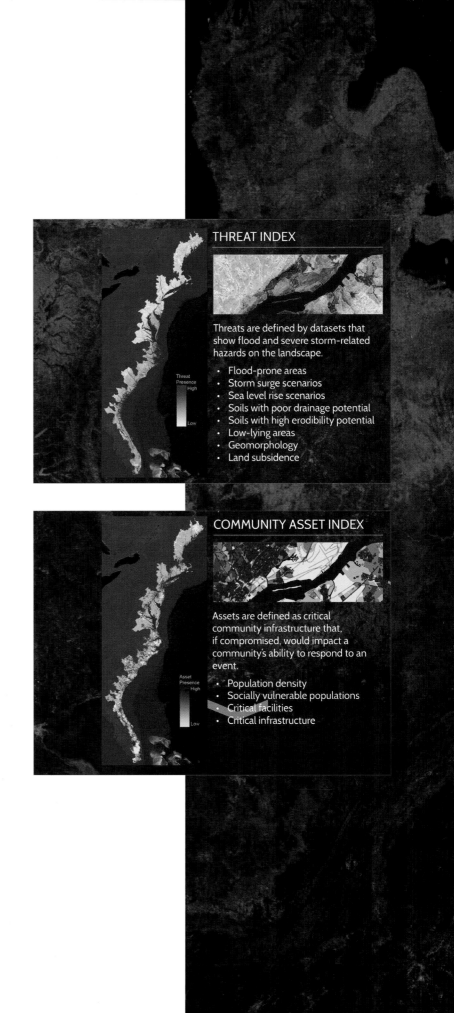

THREAT INDEX

Threats are defined by datasets that show flood and severe storm-related hazards on the landscape.

- Flood-prone areas
- Storm surge scenarios
- Sea level rise scenarios
- Soils with poor drainage potential
- Soils with high erodibility potential
- Low-lying areas
- Geomorphology
- Land subsidence

COMMUNITY ASSET INDEX

Assets are defined as critical community infrastructure that, if compromised, would impact a community's ability to respond to an event.

- Population density
- Socially vulnerable populations
- Critical facilities
- Critical infrastructure

CONTACT
Greg Dobson, GISP
gdobson@unca.edu

SOFTWARE
ArcGIS Desktop

DATA SOURCES
US EPA, NASA, US Energy Information Administration, US Army Corps of Engineers, NOAA, Natural Resources Conservation Service, Multi-Resolution Land Characteristics Consortium, FEMA, US Census, US Geological Survey, US Department of Transportation, USDA

Exposure Index

The exposure analysis considers the relationship between threats and the presence of community assets that may be impacted during a severe storm or flooding event. Through a raster analysis, a system of ranking based on the cell values of each index is used to illustrate the intensities of the intersections between threats and assets. Areas with the highest presence of threats and the highest presence of community assets are considered to be the most exposed.

The Community Exposure Index is designed to work at regional and local scales. Here exposure values are seen for Charleston, South Carolina.

This Community Exposure Index represents only half of the overall Coastal Resiliency Assessment, with the other component focusing on benefits to fish and wildlife populations and their habitats. When combined with each other along with information on protected lands and open spaces, these data can provide information on where to best site large restoration projects for maximum benefit to both human community resilience as well as fish and wildlife.

Courtesy of the University of North Carolina Asheville, NEMAC.

Exposure

High

Low

WHAT'S NEW IN SEATTLE

King County
Seattle, Washington, USA
By Victor High

King County's GIS Center has collected two sets of lidar data from 2002 and 2016. Seattle, the county seat, has seen much growth with a construction boom over the past fourteen years. The major new projects include a Seattle library, the Seattle Seahawks' football stadium, new commercial and residential high rises, a new tunnel that will replace the Alaska Viaduct, and new, bigger container cranes on the waterfront.

This lidar analysis shows changes from 2002 to 2016. Any new building will have a positive value and be symbolized yellow-green to red and a building demolished and gone will be a negative and symbolized gray to black.

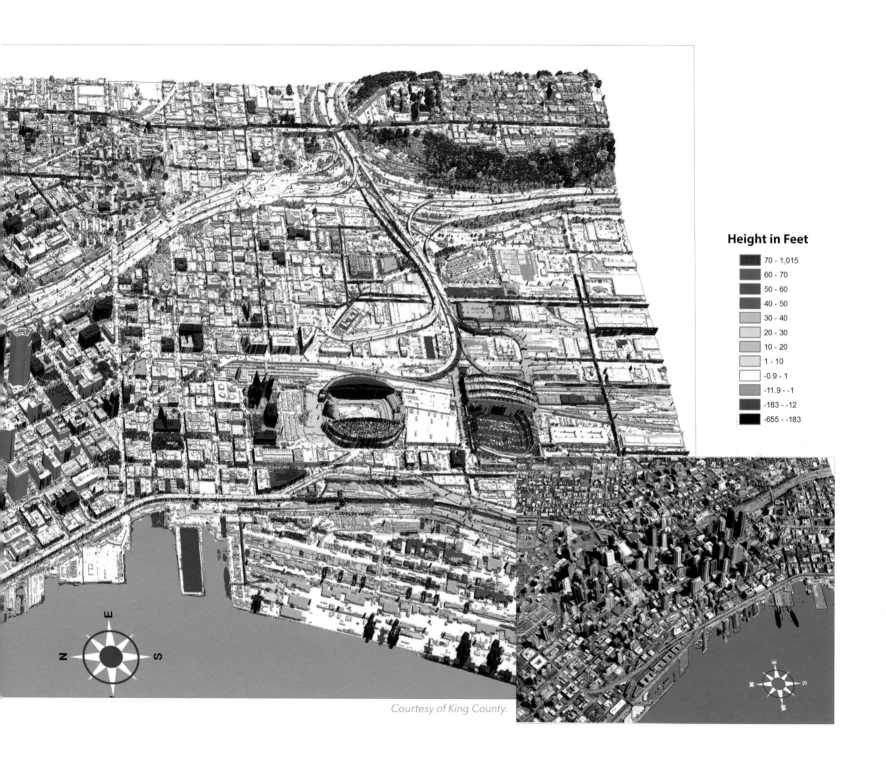

Height in Feet

■	70 - 1,015
■	60 - 70
■	50 - 60
■	40 - 50
■	30 - 40
■	20 - 30
■	10 - 20
■	1 - 10
□	-0.9 - 1
■	-11.9 - -1
■	-183 - -12
■	-655 - -183

Courtesy of King County.

No change in elevation will be around 0 feet and appear white. There are two major differences in the lidar vintages. The 2002 lidar was shot leaf off and sampled to 6-feet cells. The 2016 lidar was captured leaf on at a higher resolution and sampled to 3-feet cells. As a result, deciduous tree growth is exaggerated.

CONTACT
Victor High
victor.high@kingcounty.gov

SOFTWARE
ArcGIS Desktop10,
Carrara 6, Adobe
Illustrator CS5

DATA SOURCE
Puget Sound Lidar
Consortium

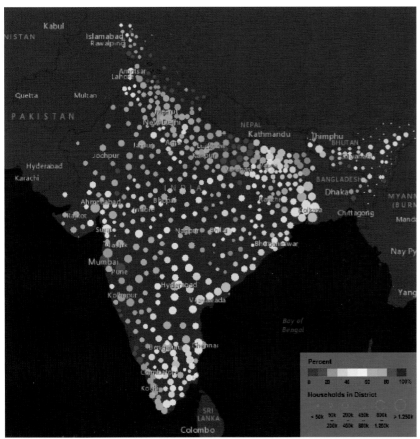

Banking

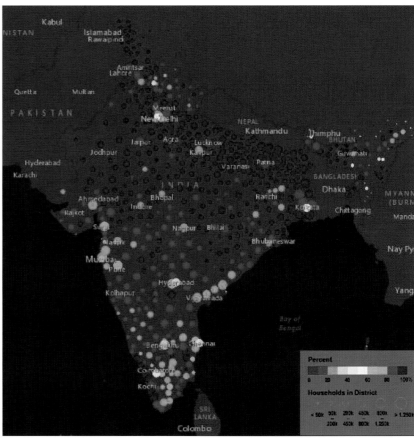

Homeownership

AN ECONOMIC ATLAS OF INDIA

University of Redlands
Redlands, California, USA

By Anshu Kishore,
Johannes Moenius, and
Serene Ong

India is the world's second-most populous country with more than a billion inhabitants. It is the seventh largest country in terms of area. The data provided by the Census of India in 2011 offers insight into how India is evolving from a developing to a developed country.

This economic atlas was a student project that provides an overview of the socioeconomic conditions in India at the district level. It is presented in a story map format, which allows scrolling through the content easily, while at the same time interacting with the maps. An

exploration of the atlas reveals that the level of economic development, as characterized by the variables selected, varies widely.

Such variables as population growth, literacy rate, access to safe drinking water, banking, and homeownership jointly reveal both the degree of geographic inequality as well as some surprising aspects about the Indian economy. Ultimately, the atlas and its underlying data can be used to inform policy makers which regions need additional attention as well as show businesses where to locate if they are interested in entering the Indian market.

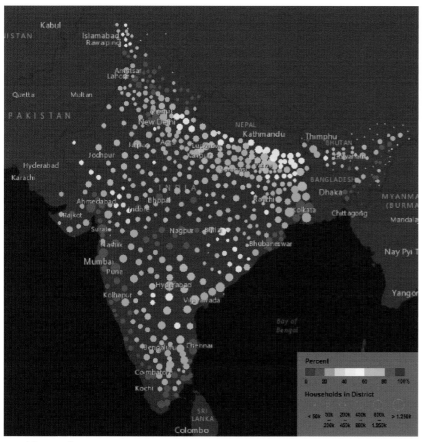

Literacy Rate

Population Growth

CONTACT
Serene Ong
song@iseapublish.com

SOFTWARE
ArcGIS Desktop 10.3.1

DATA SOURCE
Economic Census of India 2011

SAN DIEGO REGION 2017 EXISTING GENERALIZED LAND USE

Traditionally at the San Diego Association of Governments (SANDAG), San Diego's regional planning agency, a map of the most current existing land use hangs in the boardroom to serve as reference for decision-makers and the public. It is based on the sub-parcel level land-base feature class, Landcore, which has been continuously updated by GIS staff since 1990. The primary purpose for maintaining such detailed land-use information is as input for the agency's land-use modeling and forecasting efforts which are the basis for its Regional Comprehensive Plan.

To generate a readable map at a regional scale from SANDAG's sub-parcel level data, it was necessary to collapse 122 specific land-use categories into twenty general land-use categories and remove road right-of-ways and extraneous details from the polygons until the layer was suitable for display. GIS staff also overlaid the most current tribal boundaries, collected generalized land use from surrounding planning agencies, incorporated topographic and bathymetric data, and included ten levels of annotation for orientation purposes.

San Diego Association of Governments (SANDAG)
San Diego, California, USA
By Rachael Rider and Andy Gordon

CONTACT
Rachael Rider
rachael.rider@sandag.org

SOFTWARE
ArcGIS Desktop 10

DATA SOURCES
SanGIS landbase, SANDAG Landcore, San Diego County Assessor's Master Property Records file, Cleveland National Forest, Bureau of Land Management, California State Parks

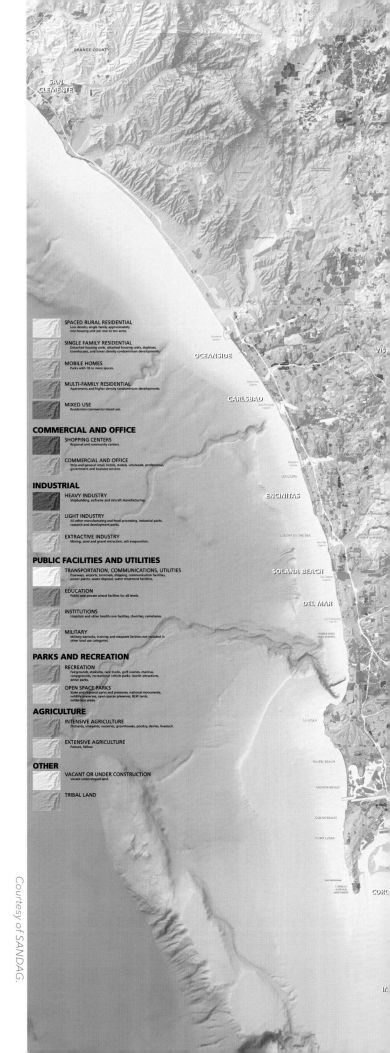

Courtesy of SANDAG.

INDONESIA GEOSPATIAL PORTAL

Badan Informasi Geospasial (Indonesian Geospatial Information Agency)
Cibinong, Bogor, Indonesia
By Indonesian Geospatial Information Agency

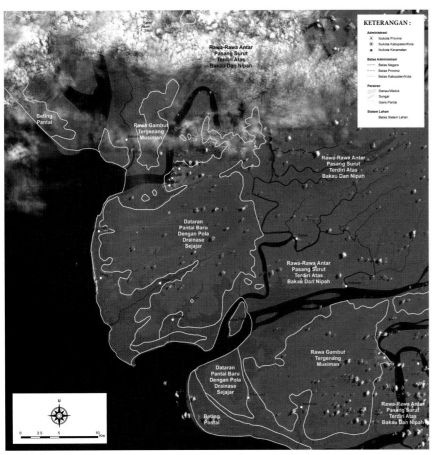

Indonesia is a large country in terms of area, population, natural resources, and culture. Indonesia also is located at a very strategic geographical position. To build this large and strategic country, comprehensive planning supported by complete, up-to-date, reliable spatial data and information is needed.

The Indonesian Geospatial Information Agency is responsible for implementing the nation's one-map policy. In 2010, the president of Indonesia stated that Indonesia should have a single referenced map so there would not be different spatial data for country development.

The Indonesia Geospatial Portal was built by various ministries and institutions as well as

local government. This system integrates several applications from the ArcGIS platform and open sources. Esri Geoportal 2.5 functions as a data collector so that users can easily search for information. The maps shown here include coastal plains, coastal swamp areas, and foothills with alluvial fans.

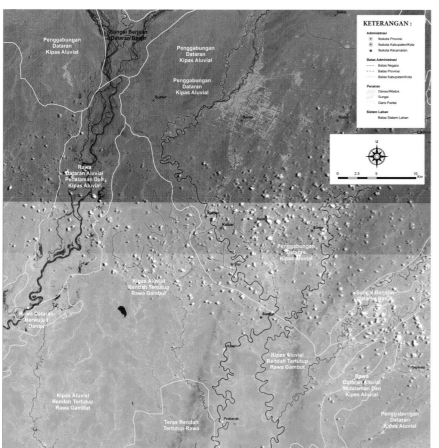

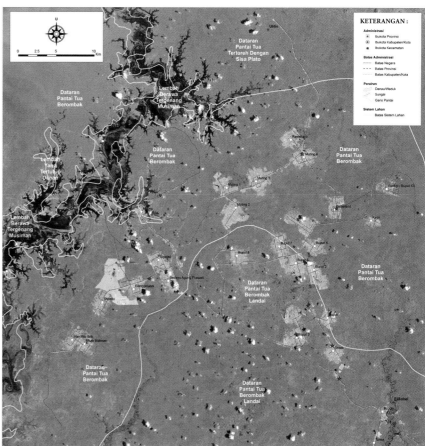

CONTACT
Ing Khafid
khafid@big.go.id

SOFTWARE
ArcGIS® Enterprise 10.5

DATA SOURCE
Badan Informasi Geospasial

NEW LABORATORY SITE SELECTION

Inland Empire Health Plan (IEHP) is a not-for-profit, rapidly growing Medi-Cal and Medicare health plan in California. With a network of over 5,000 providers and more than 1,800 employees, IEHP serves over 1.2 million residents of the Riverside and San Bernardino counties who are enrolled in Medi-Cal or Cal MediConnect (Medicare).

These maps helped to identify gaps in service within the current laboratory network and detect areas of opportunity for a new location that would have the greatest impact on IEHP Membership. The final site selection in Fontana will have a potential to service over 75,000 members. The new laboratory location is currently in development and will have the ability to support a large portion of the San Bernardino County membership.

Inland Empire Health Plan (IEHP)
Rancho Cucamonga, California, USA
By Darren Moser, Eric Dick, Debbie Canning and Freddy Ochoa

CONTACTS
Darren Moser
moser-d@iehp.org
Eric Dick
dick-e@iehp.org

SOFTWARE
ArcGIS Desktop 10.3,
Affinity Photo, Affinity Designer

DATA SOURCE
IEHP

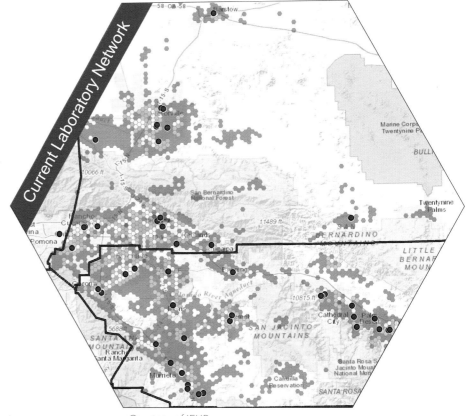

Courtesy of IEHP.

Current Lab Service Area

California

Proposed Site Service Area

New Lab Site Selection

Proposed Chino Hills Site

Proposed Fontana Site

Proposed Chino Hills Site Member Impact 2,500

Proposed Fontana Site Member Impact 75,000

Selected Fontana Site Member Impact 75,000

IEHP Membership Density
Members Per Sq. Mile

15 - 200
201 - 650
651 - 1,500
1,501 - 2,500
2,501 - 4,456

County Border

Current and Proposed Sites
Lab Locations & Service Areas

Current Lab Location
Current Service Area
Chino Hills: Proposed Site
Chino Hills: Service Area
Fontana: Proposed Site
Fontana: Service Area

HEALTH FACTORS RELATING TO OBESITY IN THE CONTINENTAL UNITED STATES

Obesity has become a major health issue in the United States. This map was created to compare four health factors (diabetes, food insecurity, children in poverty, and lack of exercise access) which are commonly thought to affect obesity. The idea is that counties can look at the map and identify ways to improve the health of citizens in their communities. While the five maps enable the viewer to better visualize the data in an easy-to-read way, the project also included scatter plots to show the correlations between the individual variables and obesity.

National 4-H GIS/GPS Leadership Team
By Amanda Huggins, Austin Ramsey, Elizabeth Sutphin, Andres Alvarez, Edward DeWane, Sean Flynn, Isaac Gichuru, Liam McCormick, Ruben McWilliams, and Griffin Winkle

CONTACT
Amanda Huggins
nat4hgis@gmail.com

SOFTWARE
ArcGIS Pro

DATA SOURCE
countyhealthrankings.org

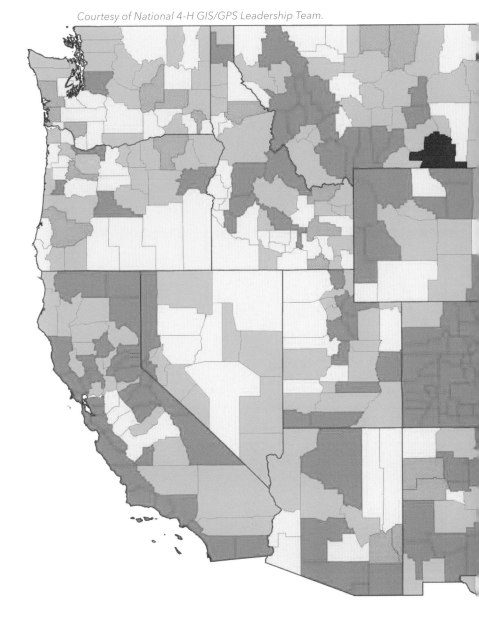

Courtesy of National 4-H GIS/GPS Leadership Team.

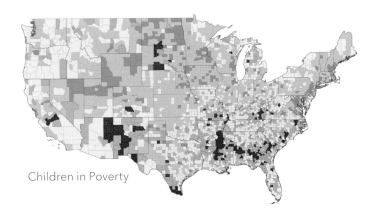

Children in Poverty

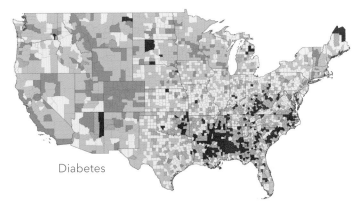

Diabetes

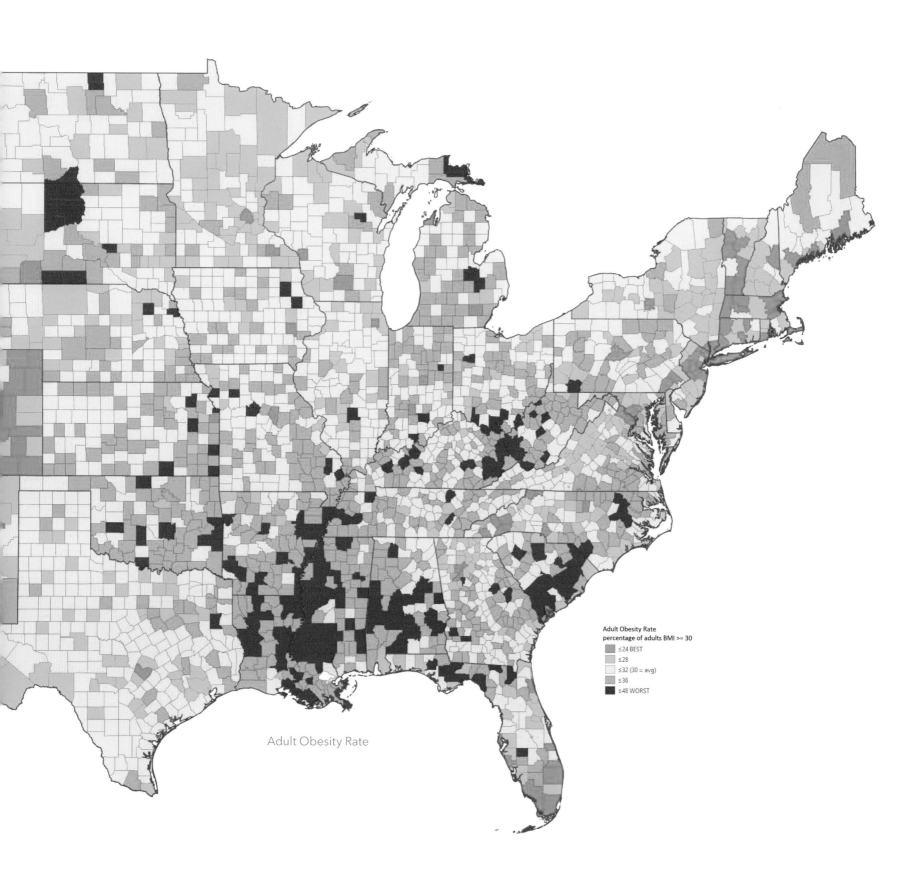

Adult Obesity Rate

Adult Obesity Rate
percentage of adults BMI >= 30

≤24 BEST
≤28
≤32 (30 = avg)
≤36
≤48 WORST

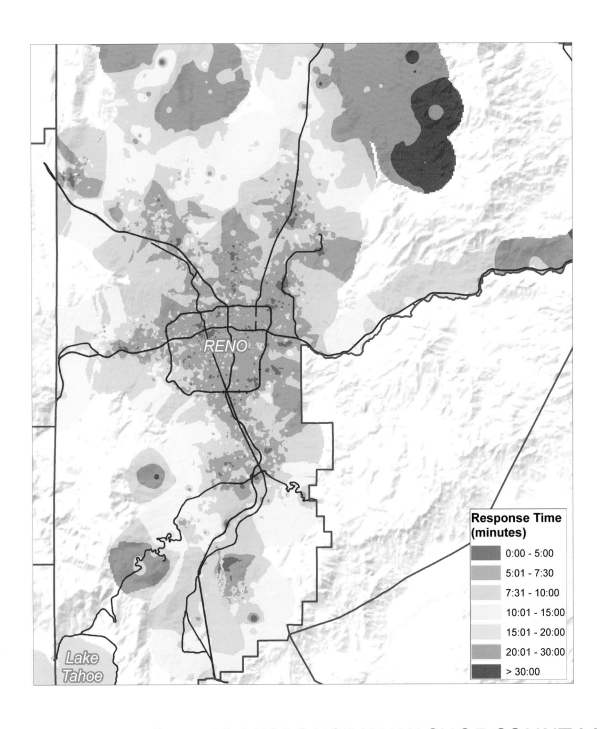
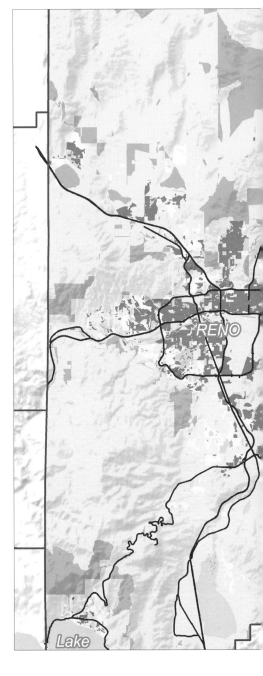

Response Time (minutes)

- 0:00 - 5:00
- 5:01 - 7:30
- 7:31 - 10:00
- 10:01 - 15:00
- 15:01 - 20:00
- 20:01 - 30:00
- > 30:00

HEAT MAP OF EMS RESPONSE IN WASHOE COUNTY, NEVADA

Washoe County
Reno, Nevada, USA
By Jay L. Johnson,
GISP, CMS

How quickly does medical assistance get to a person in need? This story map illustrates the response times for emergency medical services (EMS) in Washoe County, Nevada. Together with maps showing population density and ambulance response zones, these response time heat maps help the Washoe County EMS Oversight Program, its stakeholders, and the public better understand the characteristics of EMS service delivery in the community. The Reno/Sparks metropolitan region has the highest population density and is where 80 percent of EMS needs occur. A swipe app allows users to investigate the difference between daytime and nighttime response times.

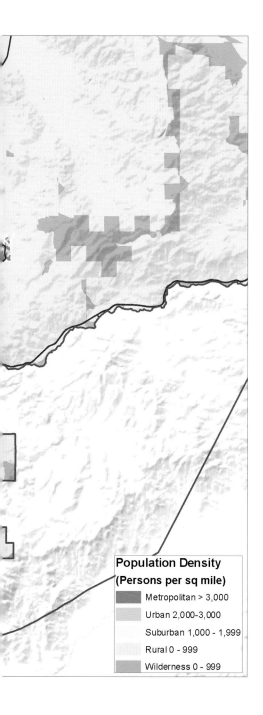

Population Density
(Persons per sq mile)

- Metropolitan > 3,000
- Urban 2,000-3,000
- Suburban 1,000 - 1,999
- Rural 0 - 999
- Wilderness 0 - 999

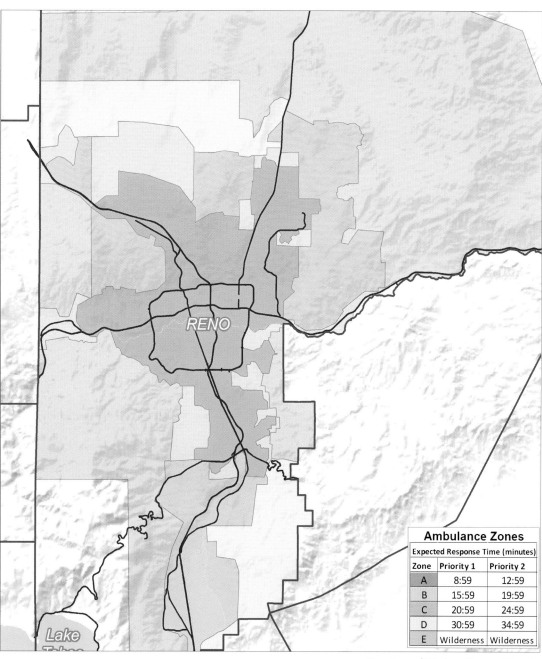

RENO

Lake Tahoe

Ambulance Zones

	Expected Response Time (minutes)	
Zone	Priority 1	Priority 2
A	8:59	12:59
B	15:59	19:59
C	20:59	24:59
D	30:59	34:59
E	Wilderness	Wilderness

Courtesy of Washoe County, Nevada.

The heat maps in this series were created from 911 emergency calls for service (points). Each point contained a time value, in minutes, indicating how long it took an EMS responder to reach that location. The times are calculated from the moment a 911 call taker answered the phone until the first responder arrived on scene.

CONTACT
Jay L. Johnson
johnsonj-gis@hotmail.com

SOFTWARE
ArcGIS Desktop 10.3

DATA SOURCES
Washoe County Health District, Regional Emergency Medical Services Agency, US Census Bureau

MAPPING GEOGRAPHIC ACCESSIBILITY TO HEALTH FACILITIES IN HAITI

United Nations Children's Fund (UNICEF)
New York, New York, USA
By Rocco Panciera

Mapping and analysis of spatial information on health infrastructure, population distribution, and the environment can complement and strengthen routine health information systems and provide better data for decision-making. This map presents an example of such an application that uses GIS to assess physical accessibility to health facilities in Haiti.

Health care accessibility delivery points is a key determinant of the coverage achieved by health care services. Natural barriers such as rugged terrain, remoteness, water bodies, and rivers can pose significant obstacles and delays for both the population in need of health service, as well as health workers who perform outreach activities in communities. Accurate mapping of the geographic accessibility to and from the health service delivery points is, therefore, an important tool to inform planning and monitoring of health service delivery to ensure that even the most disadvantaged communities can access crucial health services.

Raster-based travel time estimates, indicating the time needed to reach the nearest health facility, were calculated by combining information on health facilities location, terrain elevation, land use, hydrologic features, and road network, and assuming typical modes of local transport (motorized transport on primary roads and walking on all other surfaces). Census-based, high-resolution estimates of population density were then overlapped to the travel time surfaces to estimate the percentage of total population residing within increasing travel-time intervals.

CONTACT
Rocco Panciera
rpanciera@unicef.org

SOFTWARE
ArcGIS Desktop

DATA SOURCES
Haïti Évaluation de la Prestation des Services de Soins de Santé 2013; WorldPop; HydroSHED; GlobCover2009; OpenStreetMap; Centre National de l'Information Géo-Spatiale (CNIGS)

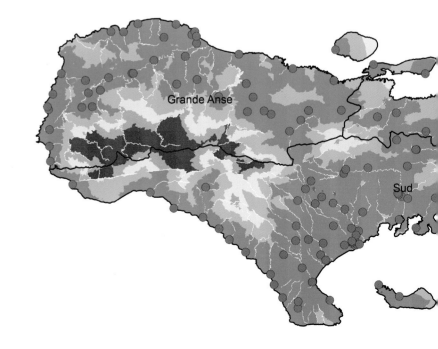

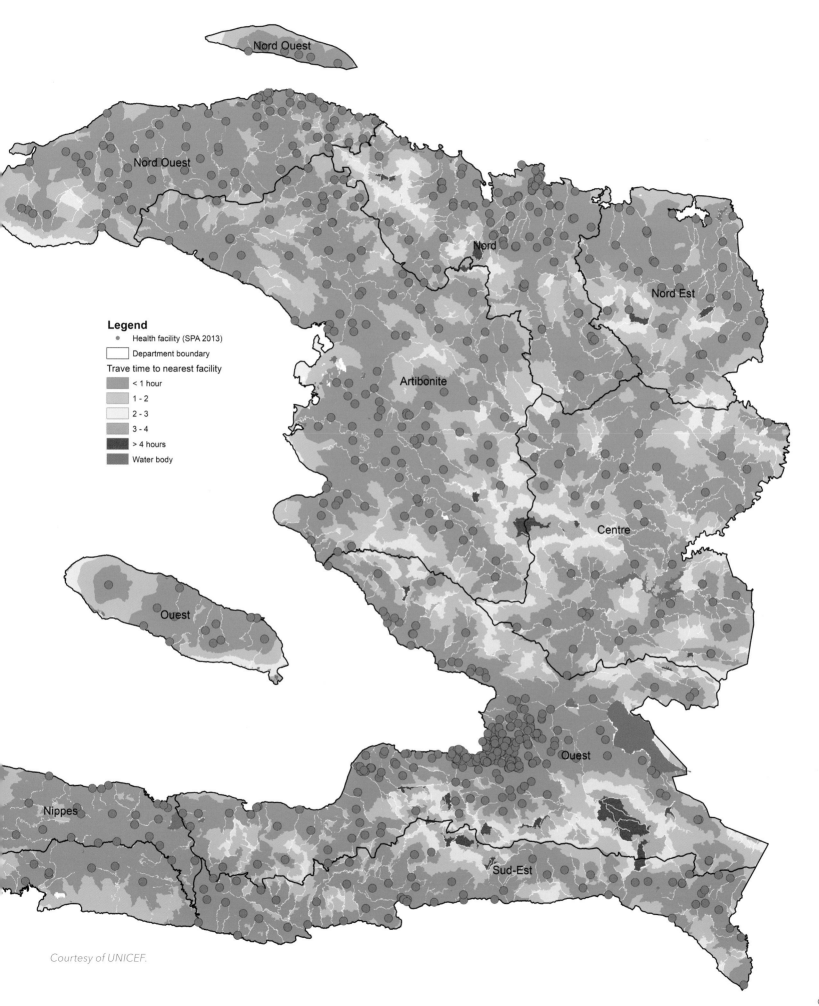

Legend

- Health facility (SPA 2013)
- ☐ Department boundary

Trave time to nearest facility

- < 1 hour
- 1 - 2
- 2 - 3
- 3 - 4
- > 4 hours
- Water body

Nord Ouest

Nord Ouest

Nord

Nord Est

Artibonite

Centre

Ouest

Ouest

Nippes

Sud-Est

Courtesy of UNICEF.

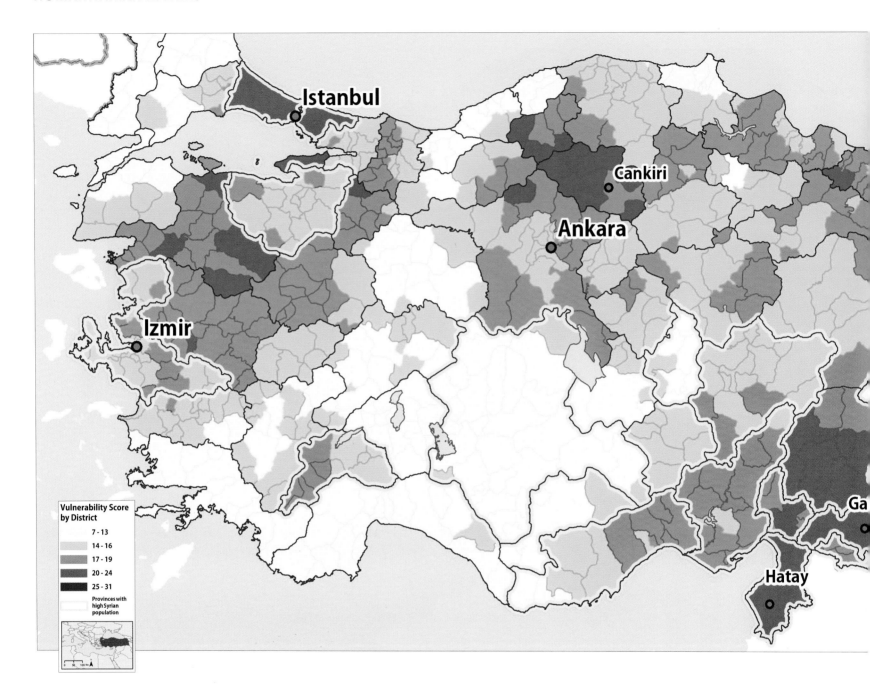

Vulnerability Score by District

- 7 - 13
- 14 - 16
- 17 - 19
- 20 - 24
- 25 - 31
- Provinces with high Syrian population

VULNERABILITY ASSESSMENT: SYRIAN REFUGEES IN TURKEY IN 2017

Tufts University
Medford, Massachusetts,
USA
By Hojun Song

Since the Civil War broke out in Syria in 2011, Turkey has become a country that hosts the largest number of Syrian refugees. As of April 2017, 2,992,567 Syrian refugees were officially registered in Turkey, and the number is still increasing. While the Turkish government was running twenty-six temporary accommodation centers, only 10 percent of Syrian refugees resided in

these facilities. The majority are scattered across the entire country.

This student project aimed to reveal areas with the highest vulnerability scores through a geospatial vulnerability assessment, and offered a valuable insight into where Syrian refugees are in the most need. To

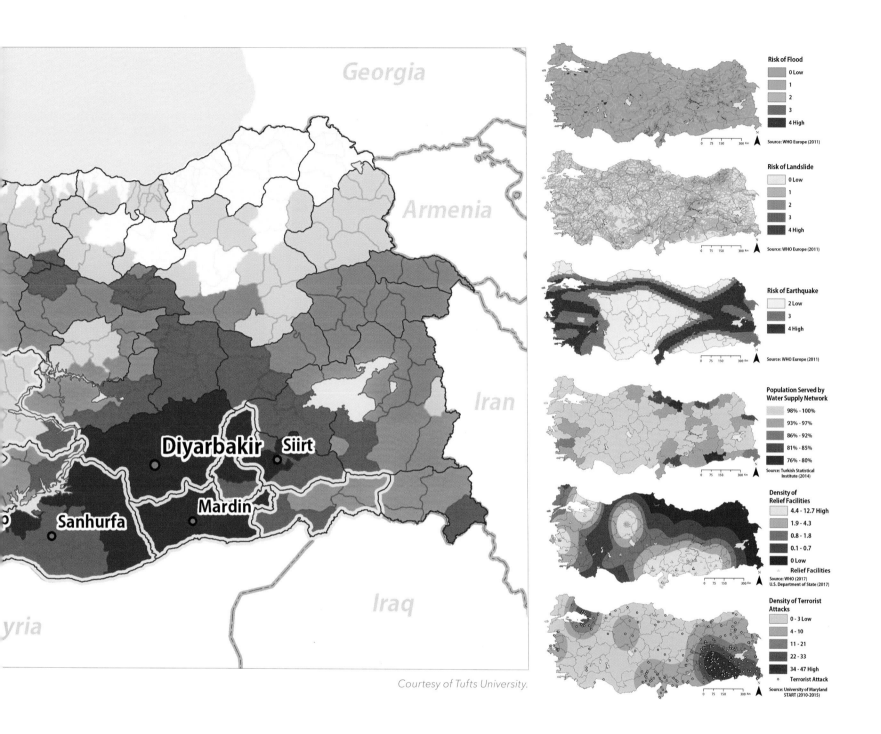

Courtesy of Tufts University.

Risk of Flood
- 0 Low
- 1
- 2
- 3
- 4 High

Source: WHO Europe (2011)

Risk of Landslide
- 0 Low
- 1
- 2
- 3
- 4 High

Source: WHO Europe (2011)

Risk of Earthquake
- 2 Low
- 3
- 4 High

Source: WHO Europe (2011)

Population Served by Water Supply Network
- 98% - 100%
- 93% - 97%
- 86% - 92%
- 81% - 85%
- 76% - 80%

Source: Turkish Statistical Institute (2014)

Density of Relief Facilities
- 4.4 - 12.7 High
- 1.9 - 4.3
- 0.8 - 1.8
- 0.1 - 0.7
- 0 Low
- △ Relief Facilities

Source: WHO (2017)
U.S. Department of State (2017)

Density of Terrorist Attacks
- 0 - 3 Low
- 4 - 10
- 11 - 21
- 22 - 33
- 34 - 47 High
- ○ Terrorist Attack

Source: University of Maryland START (2010-2015)

create a vulnerability score, eleven different layers on socioeconomic, demographic, and biophysical factors were used. The vulnerability scores of districts were aggregated, and a final map was created to show the total vulnerability scores of each district. Districts with the highest vulnerability scores were considered the most vulnerable areas for Syrian refugees.

CONTACT
Hojun Song
shj5545@gmail.com

SOFTWARE
ArcGIS Desktop 10.4.1

DATA SOURCES
Turkish Statistical Institute, General Command of Mapping (Turkey), European Environment Agency, US Department of State, UN Food and Agriculture Organization, Directorate General of Migration Management, GfK Marktfors, University of Maryland START, World Health Organization (WHO), WHO Europe, UN High Commissioner for Refugees, Emergency Services and Social Resilience

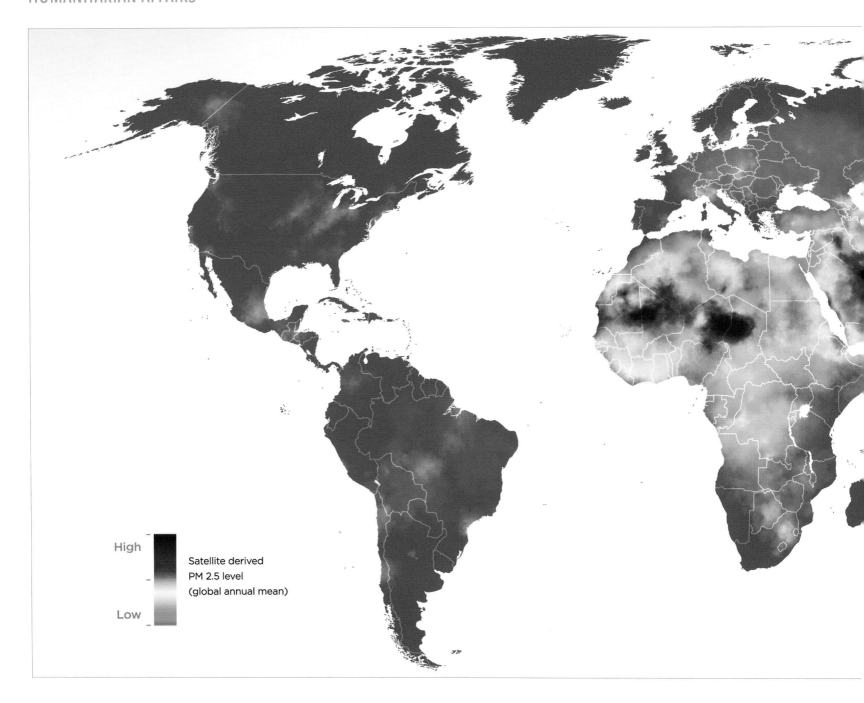

High

Satellite derived
PM 2.5 level
(global annual mean)

Low

UNICEF: CLEAR THE AIR FOR CHILDREN

Blue Raster, LLC / United
Nations Children's Fund
(UNICEF)
Arlington, Virginia, USA
By Blue Raster, LLC

Blue Raster collaborated with The United Nations Children's Fund (UNICEF) to help produce this map showing the impact of air pollution on children. In the first analysis of its kind, Blue Raster and UNICEF used satellite imagery of outdoor air pollution in combination with global demographic data to determine that 300 million children currently live in areas with toxic levels of pollution, and 2 billion live in areas where pollution levels exceed international standards. The report

also highlights that many of the poorest children were especially at risk because they have little or no access to resources for treatment and protection.

Air pollution is a critical health issue to people all over the world. Children are especially vulnerable to air pollution due to their physiology: their lungs are still developing, and exposure to harmful air during this critical period can be especially detrimental, causing life-threatening diseases. A growing number of studies are even pointing to the impacts of air pollution on cognitive development.

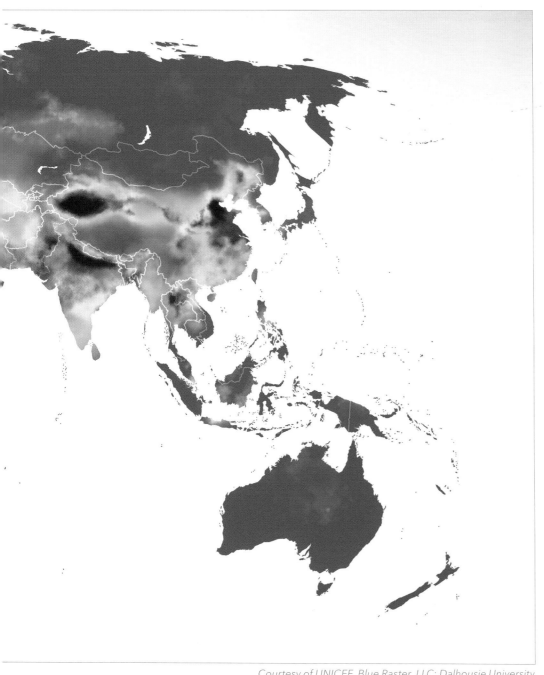

Courtesy of UNICEF, Blue Raster, LLC; Dalhousie University.

AMERICAS

130 MILLION

EUROPE

120 MILLION

AFRICA

520 MILLION

ASIA

1.22 BILLION

UNICEF has made its mission protecting and empowering children around the world. With Blue Raster's help, UNICEF identifies the children who are most vulnerable to the dangers of air pollution and promotes a greater understanding of this issue among governments, communities, and families. Further geospatial analysis can help pinpoint sources of pollution and create plans for reducing pollution in the future.

CONTACT
Michael Lippmann
mlippmann@blueraster.com

SOFTWARE
ArcGIS Desktop 10.4

DATA SOURCES
Van Donkelaar, A., R.V. Martin, M. Brauer, N. C. Hsu, R. A. Kahn, R C. Levy, A. Lyapustin, A. M. Sayer, and D.M. Winker. 2016. "Global Estimates of Fine Particulate Matter using a Combined Geophysical-Statistical Method with Information from Satellites, Models, and Monitors." *Environmental Science Technology* 50(7): 3762–72

TEA PLANTATION MONITORING USING UAV IN SHIZUOKA, JAPAN

Optimum timing for tea harvesting traditionally has been determined by farmers through observations based on their experience and knowledge. The automation of this determination process, using imagery monitoring, supports tea farmers by cutting costs and time in the field. This study attempted to develop a simple method to monitor tea-growing status and quality by using a multispectral camera boarded on a drone. The results shown here are time-series Normalized Difference Vegetation Index (NDVI) distribution maps of the tea garden in Shizuoka Prefecture, Japan, derived to monitor the phenology of the tea leaves.

Tokyo University of Agriculture
Setagaya, Tokyo, Japan
By Sawahiko Shimada, Kiyohisa Sato, Ayako Sekiyama, and Tomonori Fujikawa

CONTACT
Sawahiko Shimada
shimahiko123@gmail.com

SOFTWARE
ArcGIS Pro 1.4, Pix4DMapper

DATA SOURCES
Tea Plantation Garden, Kikugawa, Japan; Sequoia on Inspire1, Esri World Topographic Map

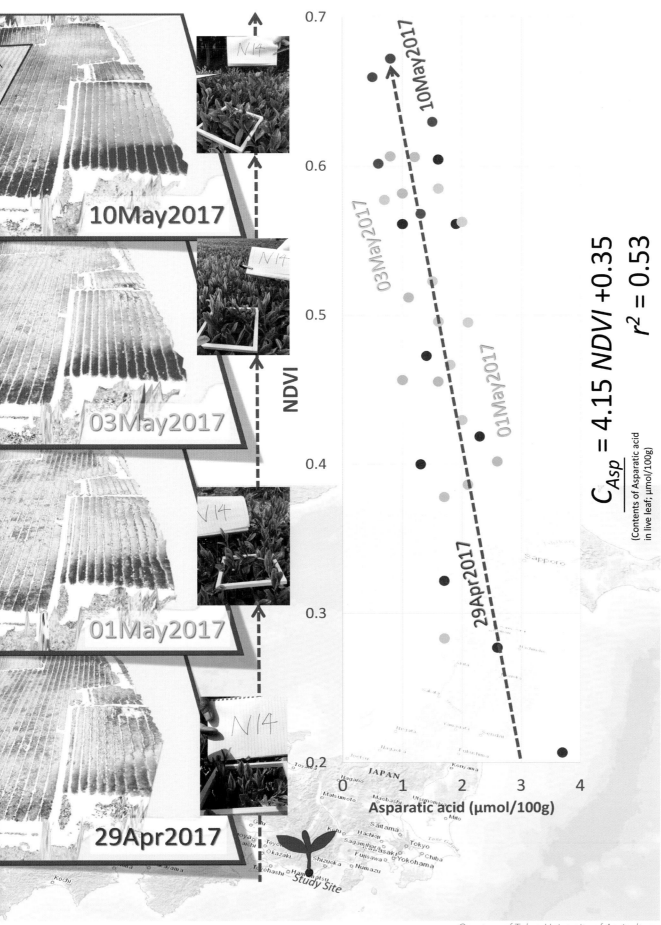

$$C_{Asp} = 4.15\ NDVI + 0.35$$
$$r^2 = 0.53$$

(Contents of Asparatic acid
in live leaf; μmol/100g)

10May2017

03May2017

01May2017

29Apr2017

NDVI

Asparatic acid (μmol/100g)

Courtesy of Tokyo University of Agriculture.

105

US DEPARTMENT OF AGRICULTURE CONSERVATION EFFECTS ASSESSMENT PROJECT

US Department of Agriculture Natural Resources Conservation Service (USDA-NRCS)
Beltsville, Maryland, USA
By Lee Norfleet, Dean Oman, Kevin Ingram, Steven Peaslee, Tony Oesterling, Karl Musser, Sharon Waltman, and Peter Chen

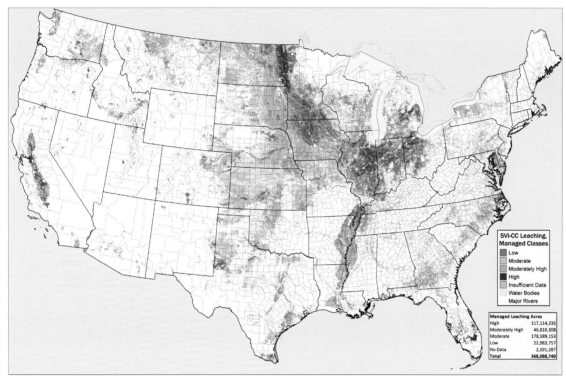

CEAP Soil Vulnerability Index for Cultivated Cropland (SVI-cc) Leaching, Managed

CEAP Soil Vulnerability Index for Cultivated Cropland (SVI-cc) Leaching

The US Department of Agriculture uses the Conservation Effects Assessment Project (CEAP) to assess and quantify the environmental benefits from using conservation practices on cultivated cropland. The goal is to report conservation effects in terms that represent recognizable outcomes, such as cleaner water and soil quality enhancements, that will result in more sustainable and profitable production over time. CEAP researchers have chosen the term "vulnerability" to describe the ability of soil resources to withstand potentially hazardous impacts of cultivation that allow losses of sediment or excess nutrients from the farmer's field into surface and ground waters.

The Soil Vulnerability Index for Cultivated Cropland is a modified soil survey interpretation. This soil interpretation uses a set of rules for the cultivated cropland portion of detailed soil survey maps (SSURGO/gSSURGO). The index was developed using CEAP modeling results to rank a soil for vulnerability to loss of sediment and/or excess nutrients from cultivation. Such losses can lead to reduction in surface and groundwater quality in agroecosystems.

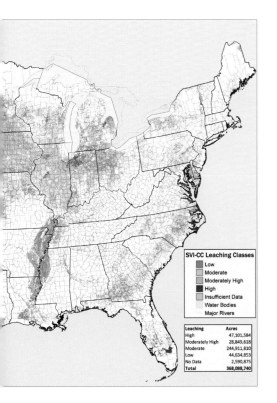

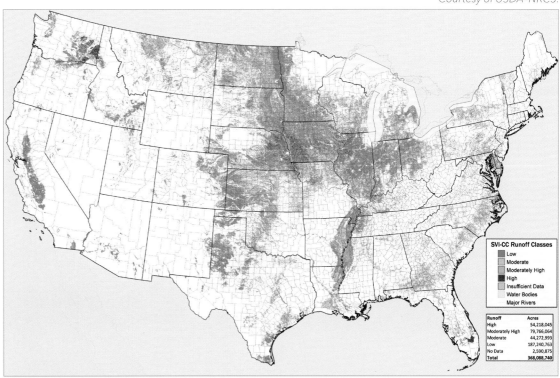

SVI-CC Leaching Classes
Low
Moderate
Moderately High
High
Insufficient Data
Water Bodies
Major Rivers

Leaching	Acres
High	47,101,584
Moderately High	28,849,618
Moderate	244,911,810
Low	44,634,853
No Data	2,590,875
Total	368,088,740

SVI-CC Runoff Classes
Low
Moderate
Moderately High
High
Insufficient Data
Water Bodies
Major Rivers

Runoff	Acres
High	54,218,045
Moderately High	79,766,064
Moderate	44,272,993
Low	187,240,763
No Data	2,590,875
Total	368,088,740

CEAP Soil Vulnerability Index for Cultivated Cropland (SVI-cc) Runoff

CONTACT
Karl Musser
karl.musser@wdc.usda.gov

SOFTWARE
ArcGIS Desktop

DATA SOURCE
National Soils Database (gSSURGO)

TIMBER AVAILABILITY ANALYSIS

The Okanagan-Columbia Business Area needs to determine and classify merchantable timber within its operating areas to sustainably develop timber harvest opportunities for the future. The forestry planning department determined the criteria for the four merchantable timber classification levels (very low, low, medium, high). The parameters evaluated tree species, their associated stand volumes, and slope. Various land-based datasets are used to create a layer that depicts the current state of the land within each area of interest. The layer is then the input of an ArcGIS model.

The model selects, calculates, and summarizes these classifications and creates reports that are then displayed on the maps. The reports summarize land-based categories by area and the merchantable timber classification levels by area, tree species, and volume. The objectives of these reports and maps are to aid in the decision-making process for planning future harvest opportunities and in the development of the five-year plans.

British Columbia Ministry of Forest, Lands, Natural Resource Operations, and Rural Development
Vernon, British Columbia, Canada
By Lynda Ronan

CONTACT
Lynda Ronan
Lynda.Ronan@gov.bc.ca

SOFTWARE
ArcGIS Desktop 10.2,
ArcGIS® API for Python,
ModelBuilder, Microsoft Excel

DATA SOURCE
British Columbia Data Warehouse
timber sales data

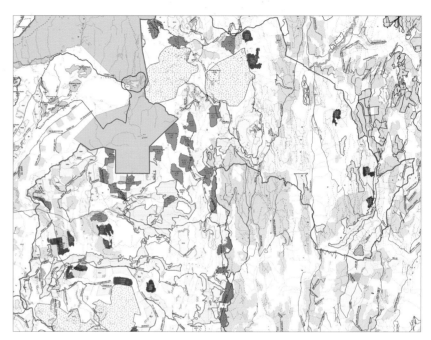

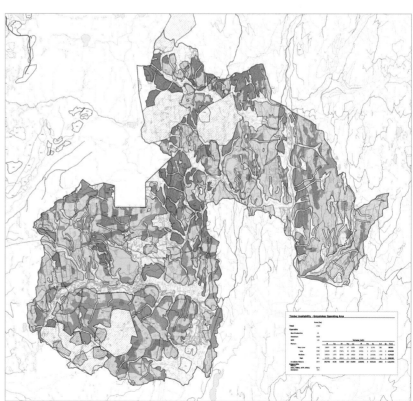

Courtesy of British Columbia Ministry of Forest, Lands, Natural Resource Operations, and Rural Development.

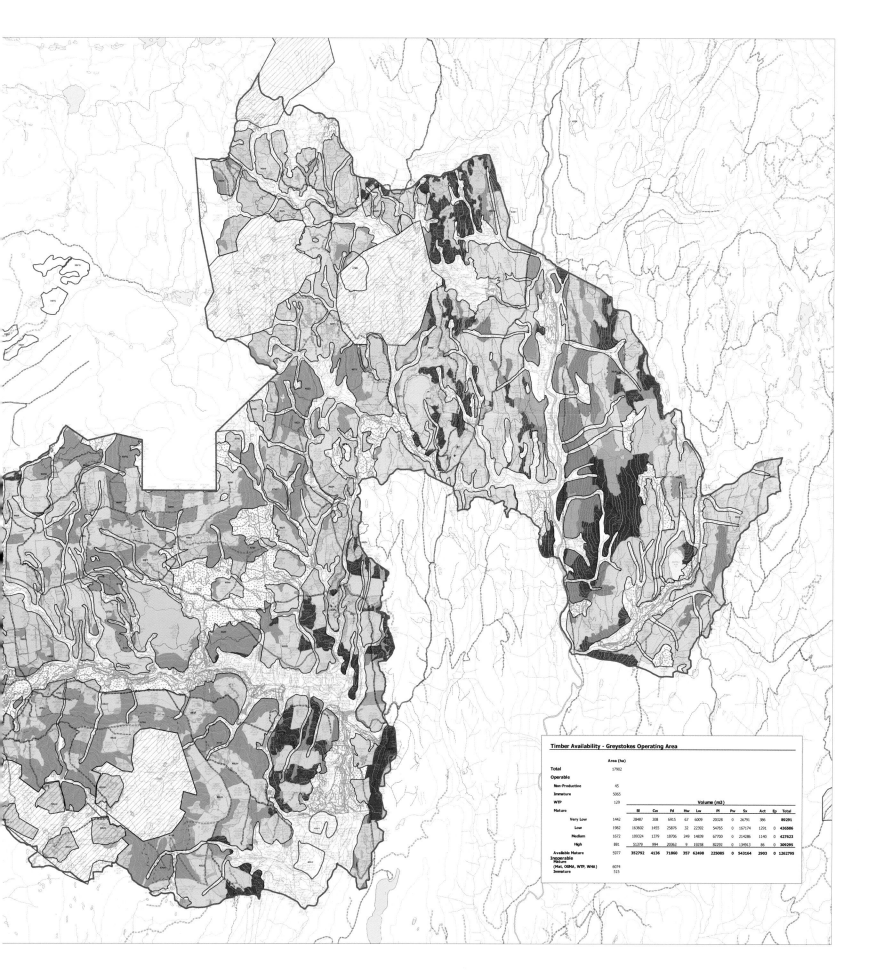

Timber Availability - Greystokes Operating Area

	Area (ha)											
Total	17902											
Operable												
Non-Productive	45											
Immature	5065											
WTP	129											
Mature		Bl	Cw	Fd	Hw	Lw	Pl	Pw	Sx	Act	Ep	Total
Very Low	1442	28487	308	6915	67	6009	20328	0	26791	386		**89291**
Low	1982	163602	1455	25876	32	22392	54765	0	167174	1291	0	**436586**
Medium	1672	109324	1379	18706	249	14839	67700	0	214286	1140	0	**427623**
High	881	51379	994	20363	9	19258	82292	0	134913	86	0	**309295**
Available Mature	5977	352792	4136	71860	357	62498	225085	0	543164	2903	0	**1262795**
Inoperable												
Mature												
(Mat, OGMA, WTP, WHA)	6074											
Immature	515											

Volume (m3)

ESTIMATION OF FOREST BIOMASS FROM LIDAR DATA

Yale School of Forestry and Environmental Studies
New Haven, Connecticut, USA
By Jill Kelly

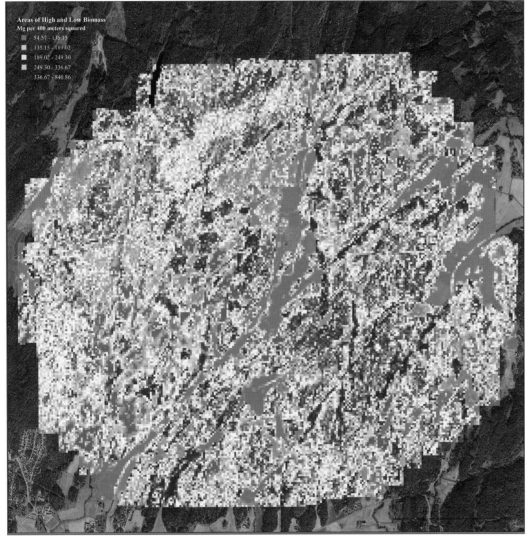

Spatially Variegated Estimation of Forest Biomass from Lidar Data

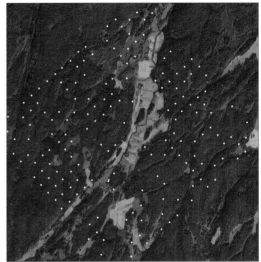

Systematic Arrangement of Forest Inventory Plots

Identify Areas of High and Low Biomass for Management

This map illustrates a method for model-based estimation of above-ground forest biomass from lidar data and its application to a small forested area in southern Norway. Statistical models were developed by relating lidar height measurements to biomass which had been independently measured on 175 inventory plots, each 400 square meters in area. The models were then applied to predict the biomass on every 400-square-meter cell that had been surveyed by lidar.

Locally explicit estimates of biomass are useful for making forest management decisions, documenting change over time, and identifying specific, local causes of deforestation such as agriculture, fire, logging, or construction. Monitoring forest biomass and preventing deforestation are important tools for slowing climate change..

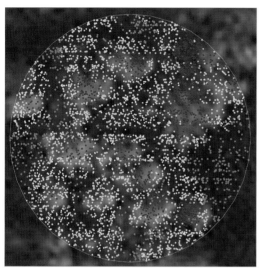

Close-up of Lidar First Return Height Points on Plot

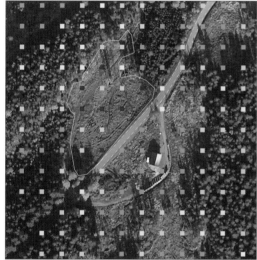

Identify Areas of Recent Change

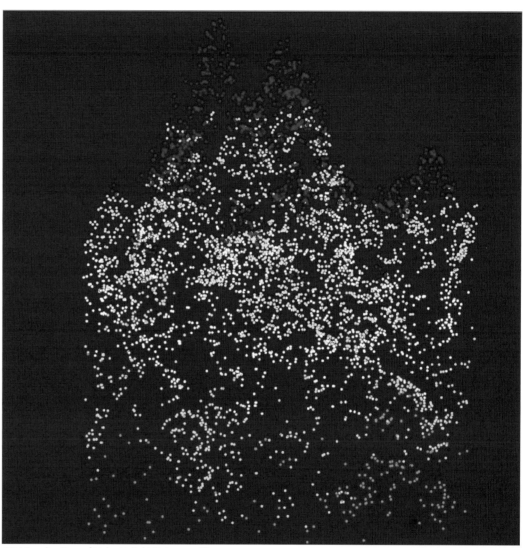

3D Visualization of Lidar Height Points on Plots

Courtesy of Yale School of Forestry and Environmental Studies

CONTACT
Jill Kelly
jill.kelly@yale.edu

SOFTWARE
ArcGIS Desktop

DATA SOURCE
Lidar data provided by the
Norwegian Life Sciences University

ALASKA MINERALS AND ENERGY RESOURCE DISTRIBUTION

The mission of the Alaska Division of Geological and Geophysical Surveys (DGGS) includes determining the potential of state land for production of energy and minerals. Geologists conduct field work and analysis throughout the vast expanse of Alaska to meet this requirement. These maps effectively communicate the division's wide range of activities along with the distribution of energy and mineral resources and as a result are prominently displayed at the Alaska State Legislator Offices and numerous other organizations.

The effective visualization of mineral distribution and activities on these maps was particularly challenging due to the numerous areas with very high-point densities. To ensure legibility throughout the map, careful attention to the principles of map design was required which resulted in the necessity to fully leverage all available graphic variables such as symbol size, shape, hue, value, and saturation.

Alaska Division of Geological and Geophysical Surveys (DGGS)
Fairbanks, Alaska, USA
By Mike Hendricks and Trish Gallagher

CONTACT
Mike Hendricks
mike.hendricks@alaska.gov

SOFTWARE
ArcGIS Desktop 10.4.1

DATA SOURCE
Alaska DGGS

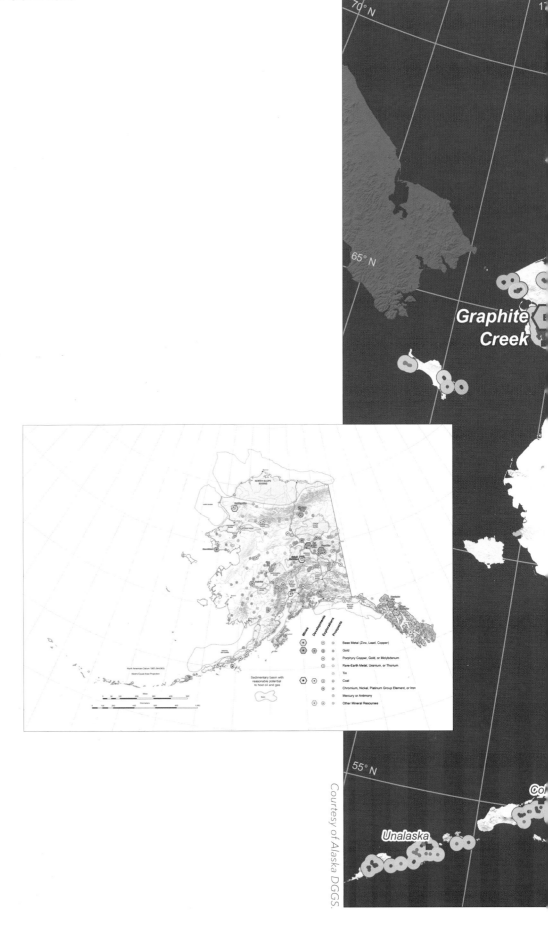

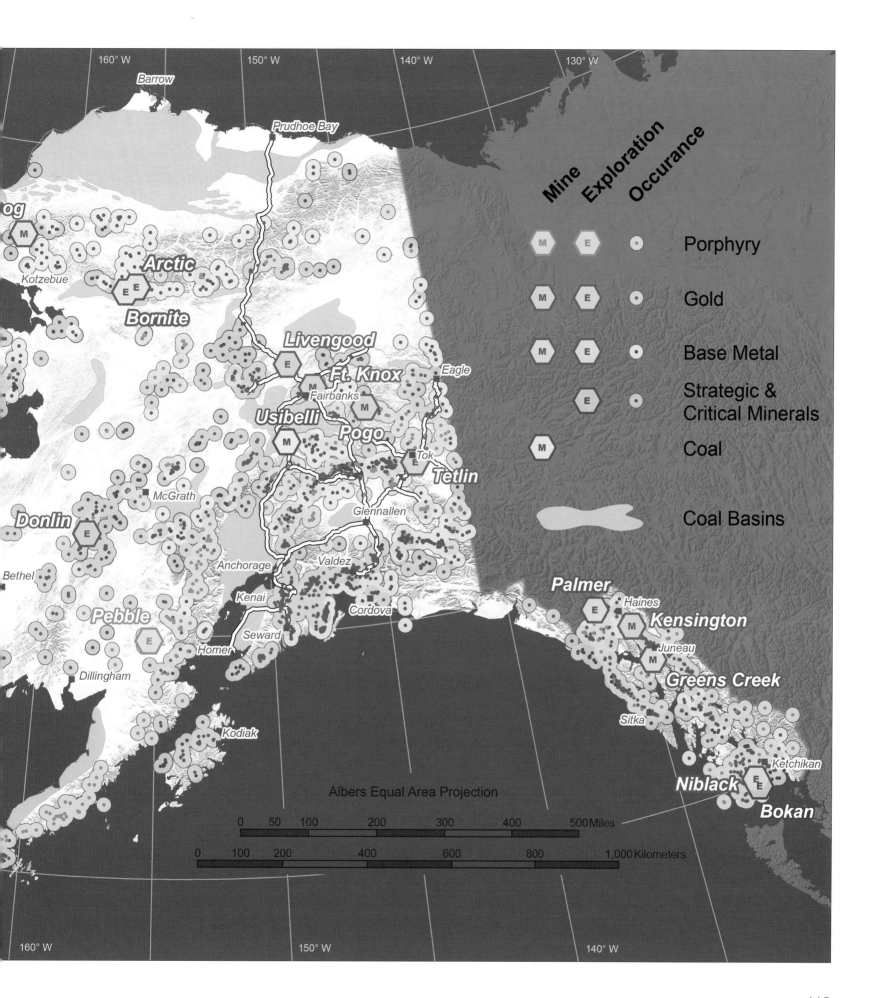

Mine · Exploration · Occurance

Mine	Exploration	Occurance	
M	E	·	Porphyry
M	E	·	Gold
M	E	·	Base Metal
	E	·	Strategic & Critical Minerals
M			Coal
			Coal Basins

Albers Equal Area Projection

0 50 100 200 300 400 500 Miles

0 100 200 400 600 800 1,000 Kilometers

Barrow
Prudhoe Bay
og
Kotzebue
Arctic
Bornite
Livengood
Ft. Knox
Fairbanks
Usibelli
Pogo
Eagle
Tok
Tetlin
McGrath
Donlin
Glennallen
Bethel
Anchorage
Valdez
Kenai
Cordova
Pebble
Seward
Homer
Dillingham
Palmer
Haines
Kensington
Juneau
Greens Creek
Kodiak
Sitka
Niblack
Ketchikan
Bokan

160° W   150° W   140° W   130° W

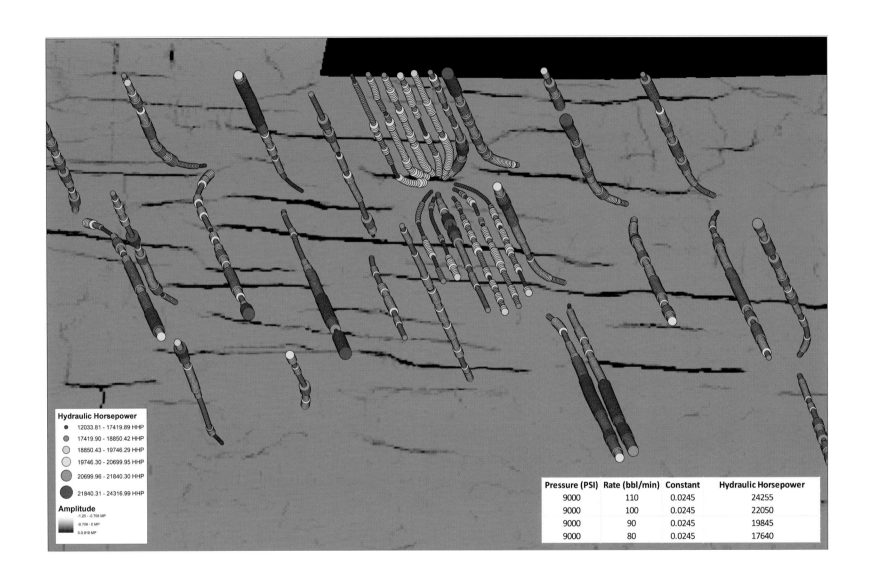

Pressure (PSI)	Rate (bbl/min)	Constant	Hydraulic Horsepower
9000	110	0.0245	24255
9000	100	0.0245	22050
9000	90	0.0245	19845
9000	80	0.0245	17640

MARCELLUS FRAC STAGES BY HYDRAULIC HORSEPOWER

Repsol Oil & Gas USA, LLC
Gibsonia, Pennsylvania, USA
By Sherry McGartland

In a development area of the Marcellus Natural Gas Play, the hydraulic fracturing stages were somewhat varied in difficulty. The task was to determine how the natural faulting of this development area might be impacting the stimulation treatments. Data from the fracturing treatment was processed with ArcGIS tools, generating several maps to see if a correlation could be identified.

Trend analysis shows the faults are impacting the stages of the hydraulic fracturing treatments. Reviewing the

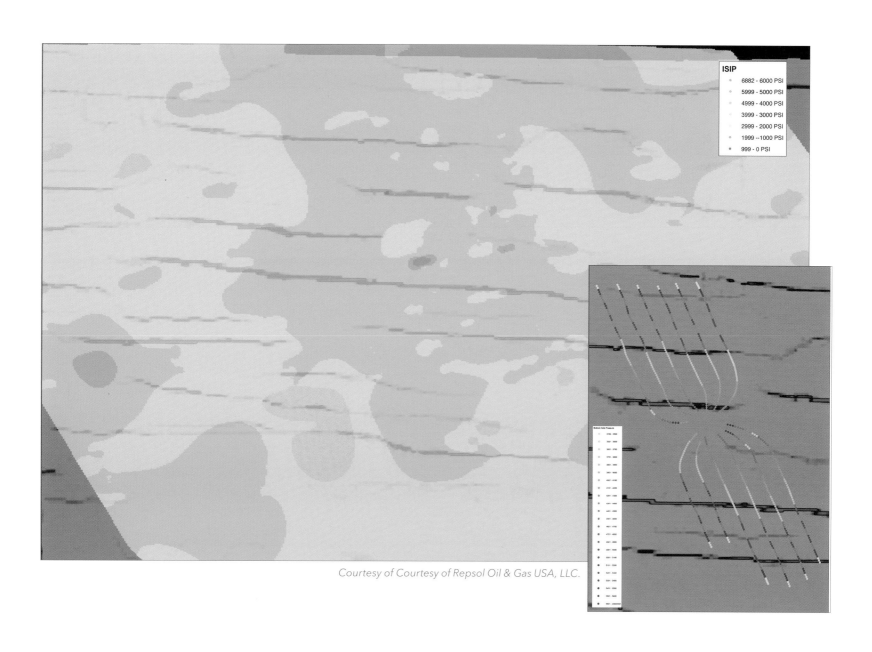

ISIP

- 6882 - 6000 PSI
- 5999 - 5000 PSI
- 4999 - 4000 PSI
- 3999 - 3000 PSI
- 2999 - 2000 PSI
- 1999 - -1000 PSI
- 999 - 0 PSI

Courtesy of Courtesy of Repsol Oil & Gas USA, LLC.

trend analysis with the drilling and completions team has led to some great dialog and interaction, also allowing creativity and brainstorming among other teams within the Marcellus Delivery Unit.

CONTACT
Sherry McGartland
smcgartland@repsol.com

SOFTWARE
ArcGIS Desktop 10.2.2

DATA SOURCE
Repsol Oil & Gas USA, LLC

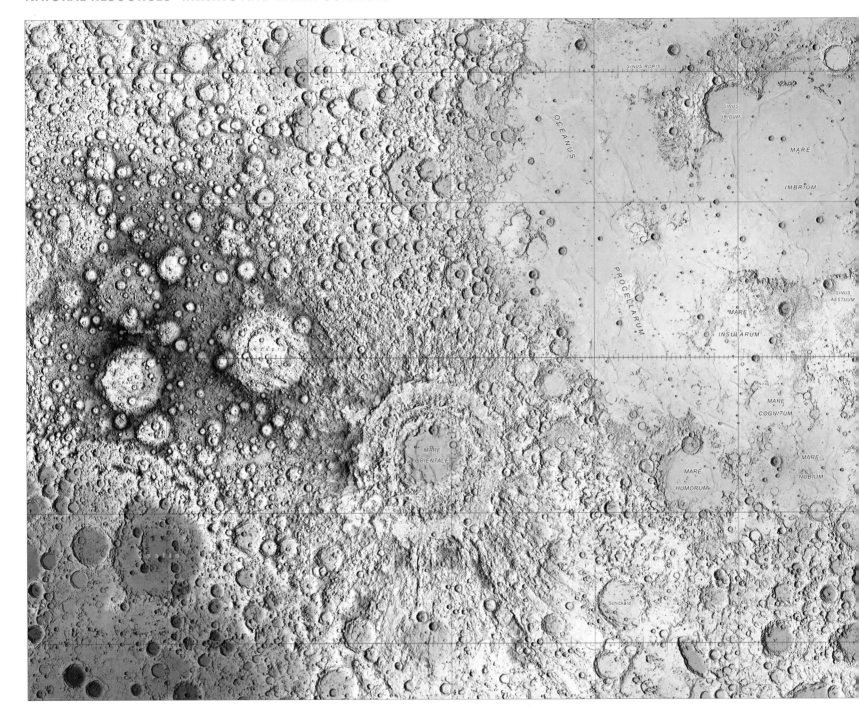

TOPOGRAPHIC MAP OF THE MOON

US Geological Survey (USGS)
Flagstaff, Arizona, USA
By Trent M. Hare, Rosalyn K.
Hayward, Jennifer S. Blue, Brent
A. Archinal, Mark S. Robinson,
Emerson J. Speyerer, Robert V.
Wagner, David E. Smith, Maria
T. Zuber, Gregory A. Neumann,
and Erwan Mazarico

The image used for the base of this map represents
more than 6.5 billion laser altimeter measurements
gathered between July 2009 and July 2013 by NASA's
Lunar Reconnaissance Orbiter. The elevation values
are the distance above or below the reference sphere
of 1,737.4 kilometers. The altimeter measurements
were converted into a digital elevation model (DEM)
with a resolution of 0.015625 degrees per pixel, or 64

pixels per degree. In projection, the pixels are 473.8 m
in size at the equator.

To create the topographic base image, the original
DEM was projected into the Mercator and Polar
Stereographic pieces. A shaded relief map was
generated from each DEM with a sun angle of 45
degrees from horizontal and a sun azimuth of 270
degrees, as measured clockwise from north with no

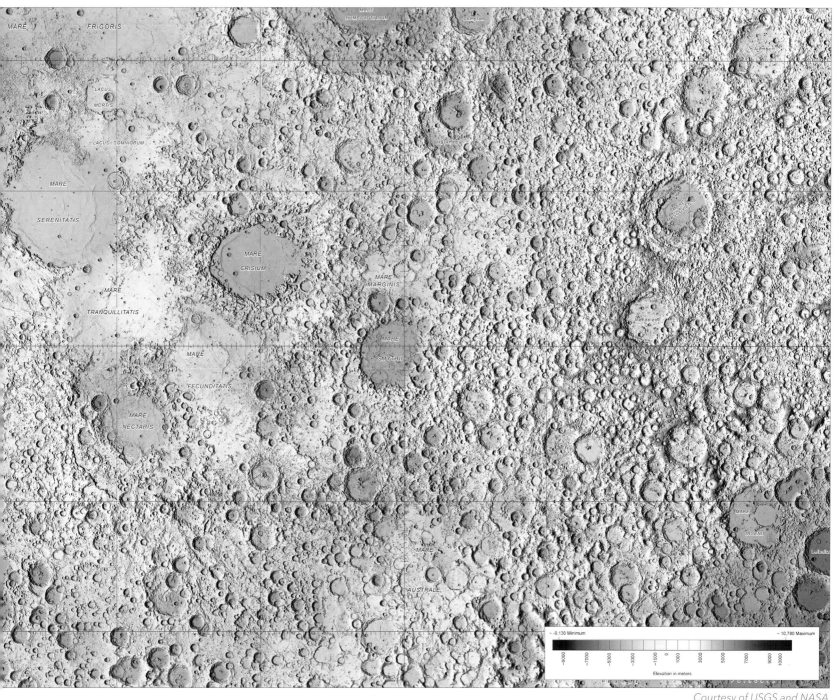

Courtesy of USGS and NASA.

vertical exaggeration. The DEM values were then mapped to a global color look-up table, with each color representing a range of 1 kilometer of elevation. These two files were then merged and scaled to 1:10,000,000 for the Mercator part, and 1:6,078,683 for the two Polar Stereographic parts with a resolution of 300 pixels per inch. The two projections have a common scale at ±56-degree latitude.

CONTACT
Trent M. Hare
thare@usgs.gov

SOFTWARE
ArcGIS Desktop,
Global Mapper,
Adobe Illustrator

DATA SOURCE
NASA, Lunar Orbiter Laser
Altimeter Team

IMAGE MAP OF THE MOON

US Geological Survey (USGS) Flagstaff, Arizona, USA By Trent M. Hare, Rosalyn K. Hayward, Jennifer S. Blue, Brent A. Archinal, Mark S. Robinson, Emerson J. Speyerer, Robert V. Wagner, David E. Smith, Maria T. Zuber, Gregory A. Neumann, and Erwan Mazarico

This image mosaic is based on data from the Lunar Reconnaissance Orbiter Wide Angle Camera (WAC), an instrument on NASA's Lunar Reconnaissance Orbiter spacecraft. The WAC is a seven-band push frame imager with a 90-degree field of view in monochrome mode, and 60-degree field of view in color mode. From the nominal 50-kilometer polar orbit, the WAC acquires images with a 57-kilometer swath-

width and a typical length of 105 kilometers. At nadir, the pixel scale for the visible filters is 75 meters. Each month, the WAC provided almost complete coverage of the moon.

The WAC global mosaic shown here is a monochrome product with a normalized reflectance at 643 nanometer wave length, and consists of more than 15,000 images acquired between November 2009

Courtesy of USGS and NASA.

and February 2011. The solar incidence angle at the equator changes ~28 degrees from the beginning to the end of each month. To reduce these incidence angle variations, data for the equatorial mosaic were collected over three periods in 2010. The South Pole mosaic images were acquired from August 10, 2010 to September 19, 2010, and the North Pole images were acquired from April 22, 2010 to May 19, 2010. Remaining gaps were filled with images acquired at other times with similar lighting conditions.

CONTACT
Trent M. Hare
thare@usgs.gov

SOFTWARE
ArcGIS Desktop

DATA SOURCE
Lunar Reconnaissance
Orbiter Camera (LROC)

HYDROCARBON PROSPECTING IN THE SOUTHERN CARIBBEAN

This Regional Report Online from Getech uses a story map to summarize an assessment of the potential effects of the end-member plate models on the hydrocarbon prospectivity of the Southern Caribbean margin. This part of the report shows the geologic structure interpreted from gravity and magnetic data across the area.

Structural features were mapped from gravity and magnetic data, as well as from STRM and Landsat data. The example shown here is a band pass of the isostatic gravity on which the structures are interpreted. Following the mapping of the structures, features were given activation histories from information gained from seismic data or literature. The structural evolution of nineteen basins are included in the study, their intrabasinal features are illustrated, and their structural evolution described.

Getech Group, PLC
Leeds, Leeds, United Kingdom
By Getech Group, PLC

CONTACT
Chris Jepps
info@getech.com

SOFTWARE
ArcGIS Online and Esri® Story Maps

DATA SOURCE
Getech Group, PLC

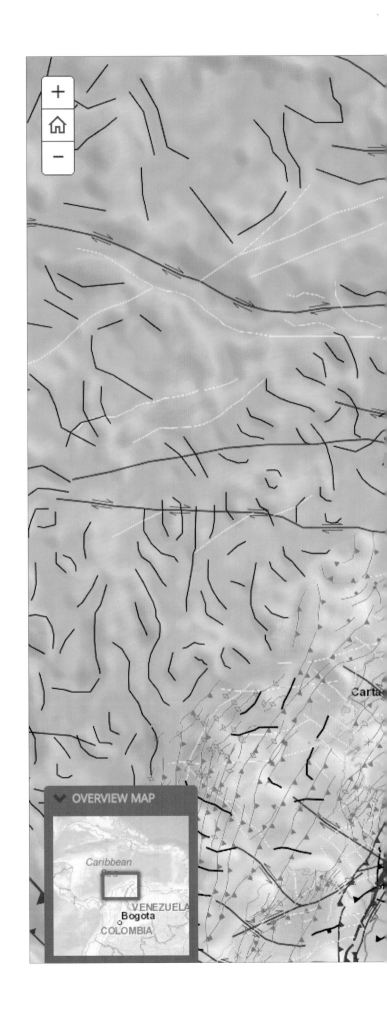

Riohacha

Maicao

COLOMBIA

VENEZUELA

La Guajira

Santa Marta

Barranquilla

Ciénaga

Fonseca

Maracaibo

Cabimas

Fundación

Pivijay

Campo de la Cruz

Mandalena

Valledupar

Rosario de Perija

Agustín Codazzi

Zulia

Carmen Bolivar

Plato

Trujillo

Valera

Magangué

Curumani

Sucre

El Banco

CHANGING PATTERNS OF WATER IN THE TAHOUA REGION OF NIGER

University of Alabama in Huntsville
Huntsville, Alabama, USA
By Kelsey Herndon, Rebekke Muench,
Emil Cherrington, and Robert Griffin

Surface water in the form of ponds and lakes is an important resource for survival in the Sahel, an arid region of Africa that receives very little precipitation. Surface water is used for smallholder crop irrigation, community water supply, and to hydrate the cattle of nomadic pastoralists.

This map illustrates the overall water occurrence from 1986 to 2016, the seasonal water occurrence for the dry and rainy season, and the decadal water occurrence for the 1980s to 2010s, for a watershed located in the Tahoua Region of Niger. The water occurrence from 1986 to 2016 illustrates the variability in the distribution of surface water, with large lakes having more permanent water availability, and smaller ponds exhibiting a greater degree of ephemerality. The pattern of seasonal water occurrence is as expected, with the rainy season from May to October exhibiting a greater surface water occurrence than the dry season from November to April, suggesting that surface water availability is largely dependent on precipitation. The decadal water occurrence illustrates the change in the occurrence of surface water over the past thirty years.

Several factors contribute to these changes in water occurrence, including land management, climate change, and changing patterns of water consumption from irrigation, pastoralists, and municipal uses. The occurrence of surface water is variable from season to season and from year to year, which can make it difficult to efficiently manage the allocation of water resources among interested parties

Seasonal Water Occurrence

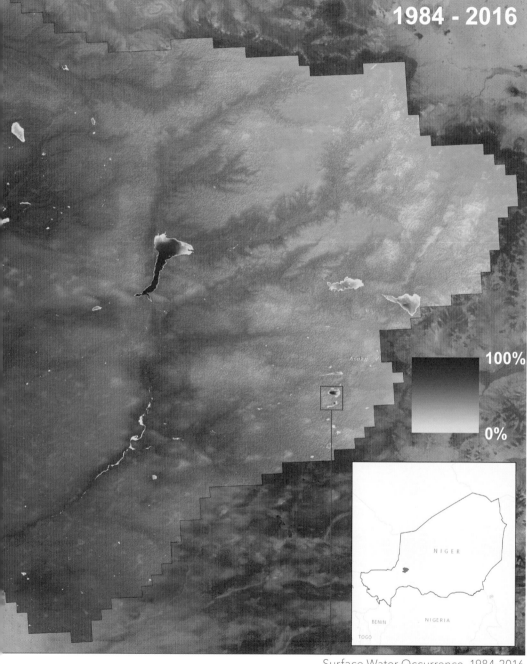

1984 - 2016

1980s - 1990s

100%

0%

2000s - 2010s

NIGER

BENIN

NIGERIA

TOGO

0   5   10 Kilometers

Surface Water Occurrence, 1984-2016

Decadal Water Occurrence

CONTACT
Kelsey Herndon
kelseyeherndon@gmail.com

SOFTWARE
ArcGIS Desktop 10.4

DATA SOURCE
US Geological Survey Landsat 4–8

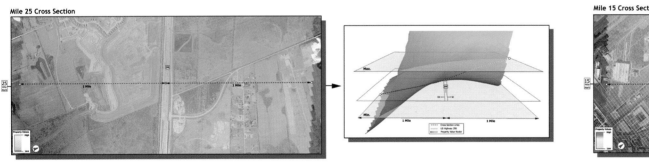

Mile 25 Cross Section

Mile 15 Cross Section

VISUALIZING PROPERTY VALUE CROSS SECTIONS

City of Houston
Houston, Texas, USA
By Larry Nierth, GISP

In Houston, it is not unusual to see dramatic swings in property values when crossing a freeway or sometimes a major road. Visualizing property value variations can be done in many ways. The idea here was to use the raster values themselves to physically create a cross sectional chart. What if the map and the chart were synonymous depending purely on the viewer's perspective? These two-dimensional locations were used to create a property increase or decrease curve for each cross section. By displaying the property value density surface in 3D (by values), viewers could interpolate the line of each cross section and see where the value surface slices through that location as a property value curve. This enables visualizing property values going up or down for each cross section of road, with increased distance from the freeway.

Houston city staff examined property values at a 1-mile-extent on either side of US Highway 290. This map enables viewers to observe and measure the change

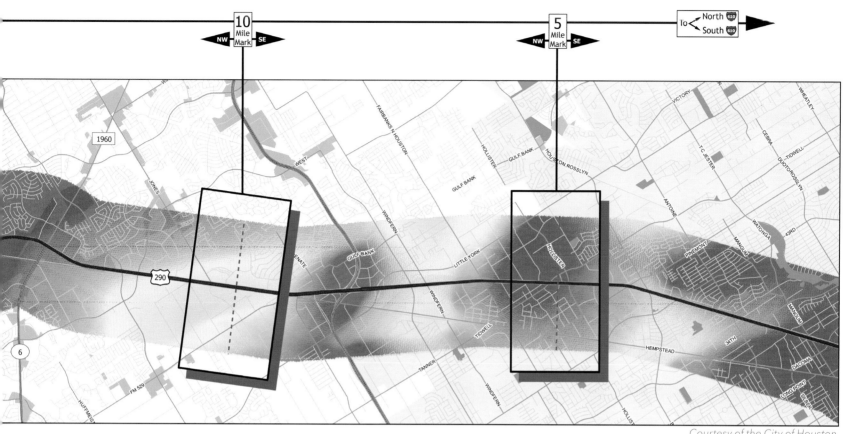

Courtesy of the City of Houston.

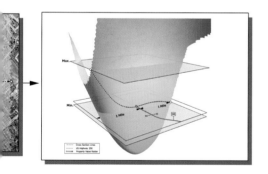

Mile 5 Cross Section

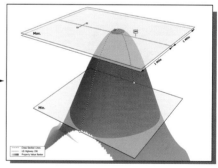

in property value densities as they traverse cross sections of 1 mile on either side of the freeway. The property value raster takes the form of a 3D floating ribbon. The floating ribbon's elevation values correspond to property value densities at actual ground locations. Locations at 5-mile intervals cross the freeway and are extruded into a 3D fence. Where the 3D ribbon strikes the fences in the air, a 3D line would be formed, represented the values along that cross section of the freeway.

CONTACT
Larry Nierth
larry.nierth@houstontx.gov

SOFTWARE
ArcGIS Desktop,
ArcGIS Pro,
Adobe Illustrator CS4

DATA SOURCES
City of Houston, Harris County Appraisal District (HCAD), Houston-Galveston Area Council (H-GAC)

BADLANDS GOLF COURSE

The map shows the original proposed high-density redevelopment project of the Badlands Golf Course located on the west side of Las Vegas. The residents living on or near the golf course strongly opposed the project and were in favor of keeping the golf course. After several neighborhood, Planning Commission and City Council meetings, only the easternmost portion of the golf course was approved for redevelopment, but at a lower density than originally proposed.

The existing terrain of the site was modified to locate the building structures at different elevations. A 3D map was created to visualize the impact of the density within the existing buildings and perform a line-of-sight analysis between the subject property and existing buildings. The data and map layout was put together in less than four hours using ArcGIS Pro 3D capabilities. A simplified version of 3D City Engine was used to publish the map to the website. The published interactive map can be viewed from any smart phone, tablet, or computer.

City of Las Vegas
Las Vegas, Nevada, USA
By Jorge Morteo, GISP, and Mark House

CONTACT
Jorge Moreno
jmorteo@LasVegasNevada.GOV

SOFTWARE
ArcGIS Pro 1.4.1, Esri® CityEngine® 2015.1 Basic, ArcGIS Online

DATA SOURCE
City of Las Vegas Department of Planning

Courtesy of the City of Las Vegas.

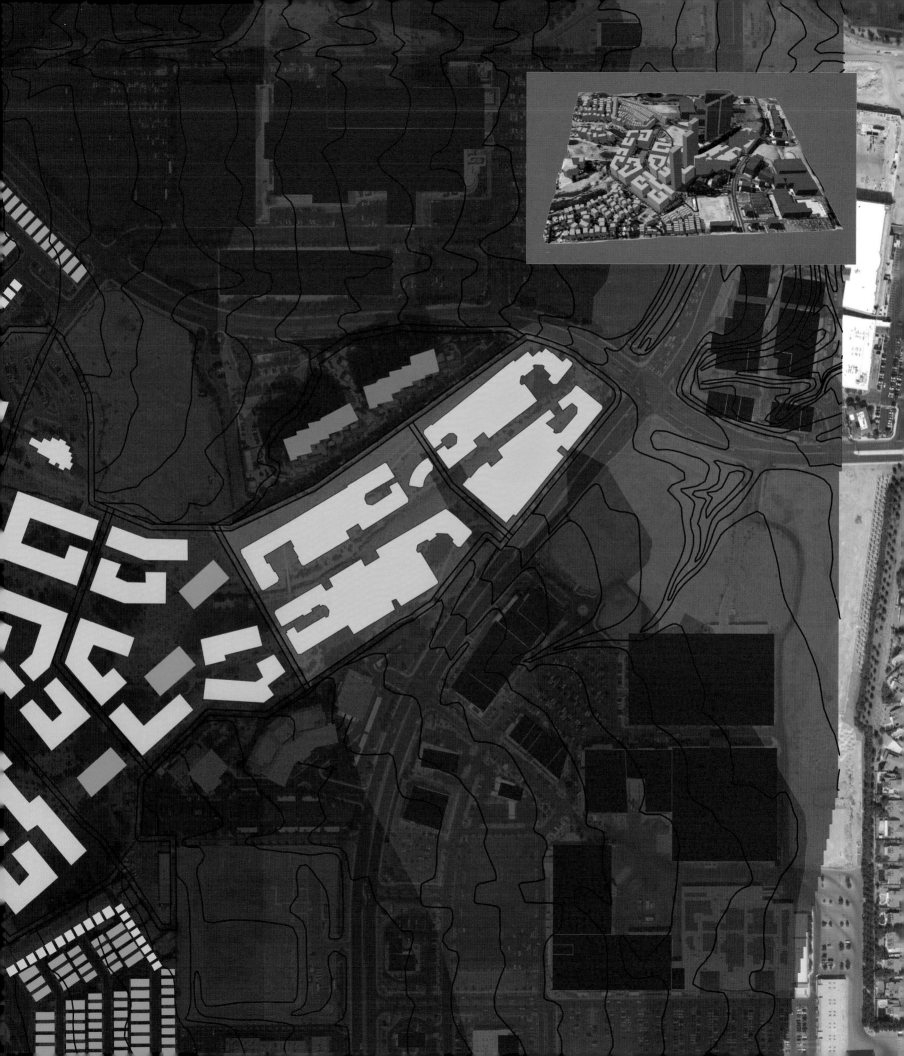

SAN FRANCISCO HEIGHT/ BULK DISTRICTS

In San Francisco, planning code regulations are often distributed geographically across the city. The main geographical units for many of these regulations are the traditional zoning districts. San Francisco has for many years had a full-sized zoning map available for purchase from the Planning Department.

There are other geographical units for planning code regulations as well. These include special use districts, area plans, and the subject of this new map, height/bulk districts. Height limits are a very contentious issue in San Francisco much like other cities around the world. There was a need for a poster-sized map of the whole city showing these limits. After a year-long digitizing process to create a height/bulk limit fabric with no gaps, cartographic work started. Traditional zoning or height limit maps will generally have a legend to refer to, but because San Francisco has 211 unique districts, a legend with 211 separate colors was not attempted. Instead, a meticulous labeling process was commenced. The result is this map.

San Francisco Planning Department
San Francisco, California, USA
By Michael Webster

CONTACT
Michael Webster
Michael.Webster@sfgov.org

SOFTWARE
ArcGIS Desktop 10.3.1,
Adobe Illustrator CC 2017

DATA SOURCE
San Francisco Planning Department

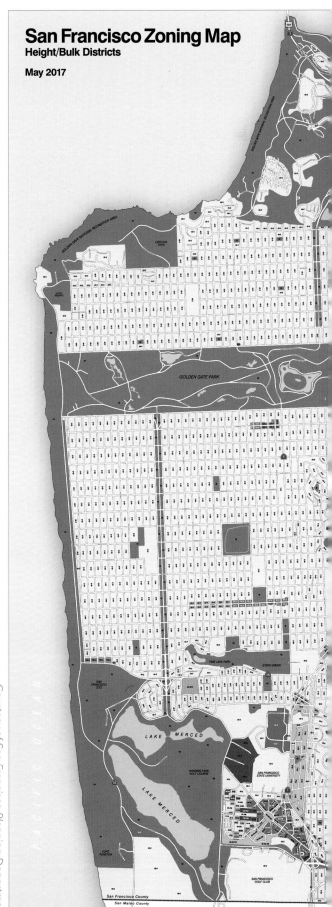

Courtesy of San Francisco Planning Department.

ANALYZING INFILL DEVELOPMENT SUITABILITY IN DENVER

Urban infill intends to promote the development of vacant or underused lots in urban cores to increase density and reduce environmental externalities associated with sprawl. Focusing on densification as a development tactic can also spur attention to and even act in the remediation of brownfield sites affecting areas of existing density. For Denver, a city plagued with low metropolitan density and persistent car-dependency, infill development may be crucial ensuring the long-term sustainable growth of the city.

This student project identified 4,578 vacant or underutilized parcels suitable for infill development, seventy-five of which were brownfield sites identified by the US Environmental Protection Agency. Most highly suitable potential sites were found to be in Denver's Central Business District, indicating that employing infill development to maintain relative levels of monocentricity may be most sustainable for the growth of the city in the long run. However, other areas of high suitability such as Washington Park West, West Colfax and Cherry Creek indicate that, with continued investment in reliable public transit and work to increase zoning flexibility, Denver can benefit from filling the gaps across the city.

Tufts University
Medford, Massachusetts, USA
By Slide Kelly

CONTACT
Slide Kelly
slidercjk@gmail.com

SOFTWARE
ArcGIS Desktop

DATA SOURCES
Open Colorado, US Census Bureau, Denver Regional Transportation District, US Environmental Protection Agency, Federal Emergency Management Agency

Courtesy of Tufts University.

Scale: 1:41,000

0 0.25 0.5 0.75 1   2 Miles

fee Park

Globeville   Elyria Swansea

nyside

Montbello

Northeast Park Hill   Stapleton

Cole   Clayton

ghland

Zoning Code Flexibility
Low   High

Five Points

Union Station   Whittier   Skyland   North Park Hill

Auraria   CBD

North Capitol Hill   City Park West   City Park   South Park Hill

East Colfax

Lincoln Park   Civic Center   Cheesman Park   Congress Park   Hale   Montclair

Capitol Hill

Tree Cover by Block
Low   High
Medium

Country Club

Speer   Cherry Creek   Hilltop   Lowry Field

Baker

mar park   Washington Park West   Belcaro   Windsor

Washington Park   Washington Virginia Vale

Structural Density per Acre

0 1 2   4 Miles

Scale: 1:173,000   0.0   0.38

N

Cory - Merrill

y Hill   Platt Park   Virginia Village

Rosedale   University   University Park   Goldsmith

Indian Creek

- South Platte   Overland

Housing Units per Acre

0   25.4

University Hills

Wellshire   University Hills

Hampden

Kennedy

Infill Development Suitability

Low   Medium   High   Southmoor Park

Hampden South

GEORGIA ARMY NATIONAL GUARD SITE SELECTION ANALYSIS

As an integral component of the Construction and Facilities Management Office-Environmental and Planning Departments, the GIS section supports and makes better-informed decisions for the Georgia Army National Guard (GAARNG). By using geospatial technology, the section develops site selection analyses to determine the most feasible sites to build a variety of facilities.

For this analysis, a suitable site was needed for a Combined Support Maintenance Shop (CSMS) and a United States Property and Fiscal Office (USP&FO). The development of the CSMS and USP&FO requires sites that meet specific space requirements. The process includes identifying sites supporting space requirements for either the CSMS or the USP&FO (one facility) or as combined (both facilities on one site). Identifying a contiguous site for the CSMS and the USP&FO helps overcome logistical and geographical constraints and allow for future expansion. The parameters for the identification of the sites are based on building and parking space requirements, proximity to other GAARNG facilities, and sites located within 10 miles of an interstate for easy maneuvering of military equipment and other property assets.

Georgia Department of Defense Construction and Facilities Management Office
Marietta, Georgia, USA
By James E. Fitzgerald, Dania Aponte, and Joel Eastman

CONTACT
James Fitzgerald
james.e.fitzgerald114.nfg@mail.mil

SOFTWARE
ArcGIS Desktop10.3.1

DATA SOURCES
Georgia Army National Guard, Georgia Department of Transportation, Geospatial Data Gateway

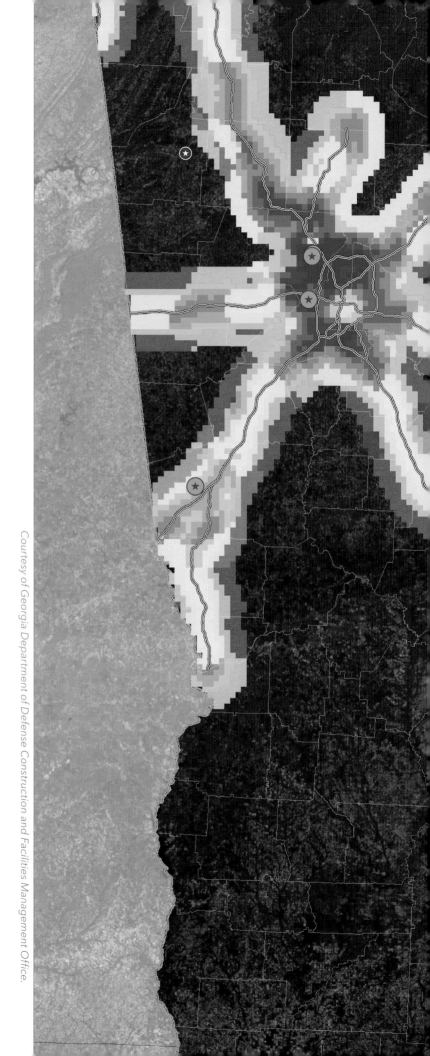

Courtesy of Georgia Department of Defense Construction and Facilities Management Office.

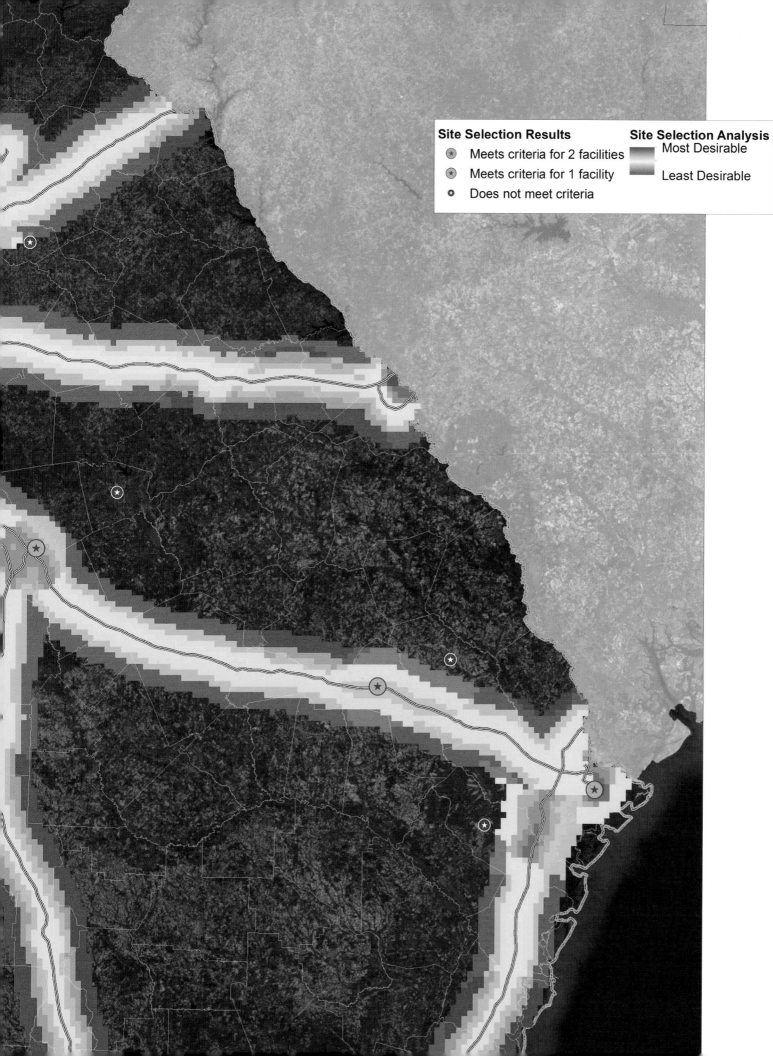

Site Selection Results

- Meets criteria for 2 facilities
- Meets criteria for 1 facility
- Does not meet criteria

Site Selection Analysis

Most Desirable

Least Desirable

133

A STUDY OF PLOT RATIO/ BUILDING HEIGHT RESTRICTIONS IN HIGH-DENSITY CITIES

The Hong Kong Polytechnic University
Hong Kong, Hong Kong
By Geoffrey Shen, Stanley Yeung, Ivy Wong,
Man Sing Wong, Jian Guo, Zhe Qin, Bingxia Sun,
Chi Wai Wong, Yuanzhen Song, and Ka Wan Pang

As urban areas continue to grow globally they face enormous challenges in terms of land supply. Hong Kong is an international metropolis, which is suffering from a chronic lack of land resources, housing supply, and the impacts of high-density urban development specially. Although several studies have been conducted to explore the feasibility of increasing development intensity by assessing environmental impacts, infrastructure capacity, and public consultation, these reviews and assessments were conducted using 2D Geographical Information System. However, most people cannot visualize the impact of relaxed plot ratio/building height (PR/BH) restrictions from a 2D drawing, since the spatial distribution of land unit in the real world is three-dimensional.

This study aimed to measure the impacts of minor relaxation of maximum PR/BH restrictions of twenty-one sites in Kai Tak Development Area from a sustainability perspective using 3D modelling and spatial analyses technologies, including urban skyline, visual impact on mountain ridgeline, shadow and solar exposure, wind ventilation, and air temperature. Different scenarios with various PR/BH for the target sites were simulated and compared.

The Hong Kong case study indicates that people could get a more holistic view and be able to make more effective and informed decisions through 3D modelling, spatial analysis, and computational fluid dynamics technologies. Considering the minor analyses, scenario 4 is the recommended reasonable scale to relax the maximum PR/BH restriction for the twenty-one target sites. The method proposed can also be applied in urban renewal for other densely populated cities.

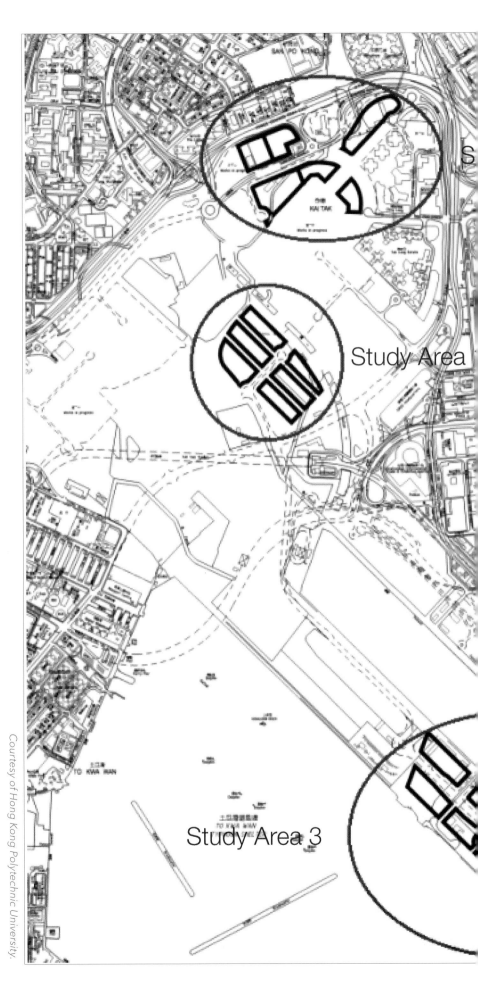

Courtesy of Hong Kong Polytechnic University.

Area 2

N↑

3D Spatial Data Collected from Lands Department

Data Collection and 3D Modelling

Sun Yat Sen Memorial Park The Hong Kong Convention and Exhibition Centre Quarry Bay Park

CONTACT
Jian Guo
orianna.guo@polyu.edu.hk

SOFTWARE
ArcGIS Desktop10.3.1,
Esri CityEngine 2015.1,
Envi-met 4.0

DATA SOURCES
Kai Tak 3D spatial data
and planning data, digital
elevation model of Hong Kong

CONNECTING THE DC REGION

The Trust for Public Land
Santa Fe, New Mexico, USA
By Chris David, Carolyn Ives, Lindsay Withers, Nickolas Viau (Allpoints GIS), and Michael Scisco (Unique Places GIS & Design)

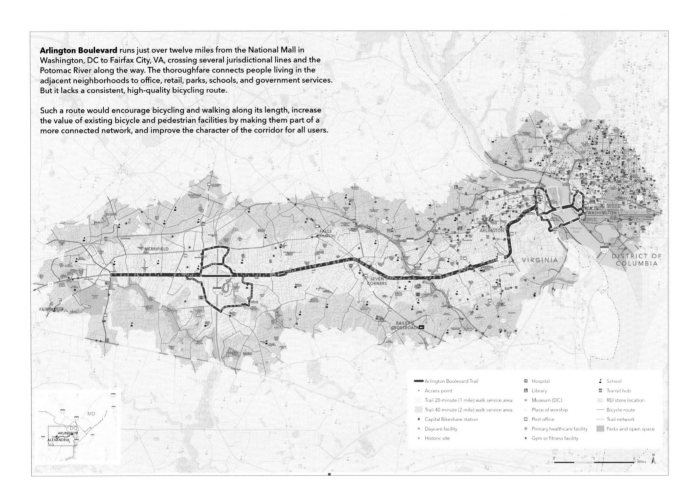

Arlington Boulevard runs just over twelve miles from the National Mall in Washington, DC to Fairfax City, VA, crossing several jurisdictional lines and the Potomac River along the way. The thoroughfare connects people living in the adjacent neighborhoods to office, retail, parks, schools, and government services. But it lacks a consistent, high-quality bicycling route.

Such a route would encourage bicycling and walking along its length, increase the value of existing bicycle and pedestrian facilities by making them part of a more connected network, and improve the character of the corridor for all users.

The Trust for Public Land and the Washington Area Bicyclist Association (WABA), with financial support from REI, are working to strengthen the Washington, DC-area bike trail system, including studying the potential benefits of three proposed trails. These findings will help WABA advocate for the strategic development of a well-connected, well-designed trail network, which will enable safer bike trips to schools, parks, and offices; reduce carbon emissions; and create opportunities for hundreds of thousands of DC-area residents to get outside and exercise.

Interactive Story Map

When completed, the **The Metropolitan Branch Trail** will be a 8-mile multi-use trail running from Union Station in the District of Columbia to Silver Spring, MD. The finished segment we have today is the result of over 25 years of steadfast effort from committed residents, advocates, and planners through a lengthy public process.

Washington, Baltimore and Annapolis Trail (WB&A) is a paved multi-use trail that runs from Maryland Route 450 in Prince George's County to the Patuxent River at the border of Prince George's and Anne Arundel Counties. Efforts are underway to extend the WB&A trail north-eastward over the Patuxent River and toward the Thurgood Marshall Baltimore-Washington International Airport.

Currently, WB&A Trail does not connect into Washington, DC. Extending the WB&A trail to the Anacostia River Trail at the Maryland/Washington DC border would provide analogous trail connectivity for a large area of central Prince George's County serving residents and visitors.

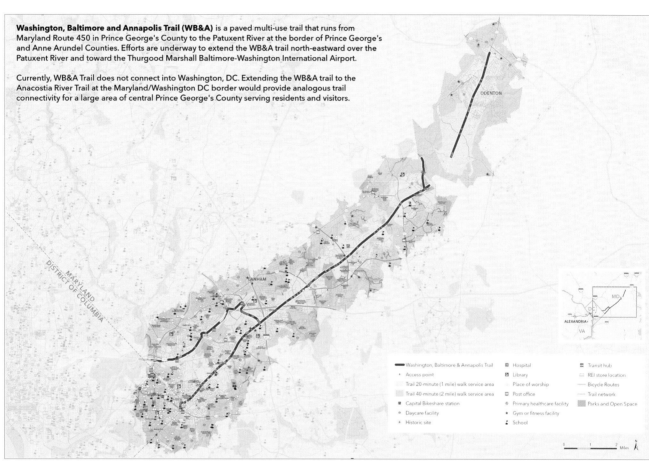

Copyright © The Trust for Public Land, Capital Trails Coalition, Washington Area Bicyclist Association. Information on this map is provided for purposes of discussion and visualization only.

CONTACT
Chris David
chris.david@tpl.org

SOFTWARE
ArcGIS Desktop 10.3,
Esri® Story Map Cascade℠,
ModelBuilder, ArcGIS Server

DATA SOURCES
Esri, the District of Columbia, counties of Arlington, Fairfax, Montgomery, and Prince George's; Washington Area Bicyclist Association

CLIMATE-SMART CITIES™ BOSTON

The Trust for Public Land, in partnership with the City of Boston, Greenovate, and Boston Harbor Now, is preparing Boston for the many impacts of a changing climate. The partnership is leading the way in developing data-driven planning strategies and green infrastructure solutions that will advance equity and make the city more resilient. As Boston battles warmer days, rising sea levels, and more intense storms, this project is engaging community members across the city to understand their concerns about climate change. The partnership addresses local priorities and helps create a stronger, more resilient Boston for everyone.

The Trust for Public Land
Santa Fe, New Mexico, USA
By Chris David, Carolyn Ives, Lara Miller, and Lindsay Withers

CONTACT
Chris David
chris.david@tpl.org

SOFTWARE
ArcGIS Desktop 10.3,
Esri Story Map Cascade℠,
ArcGIS Server

DATA SOURCES
Esri, City of Boston, Greenovate Boston, Boston Harbor Now, The Trust for Public Land

Strategic Green Infrastructure Investment Priority
High
Moderate to high
Moderate
Boston boundary
Priority lands already under protection
Parks, open space, and other protected land

0   1   2 Miles   N

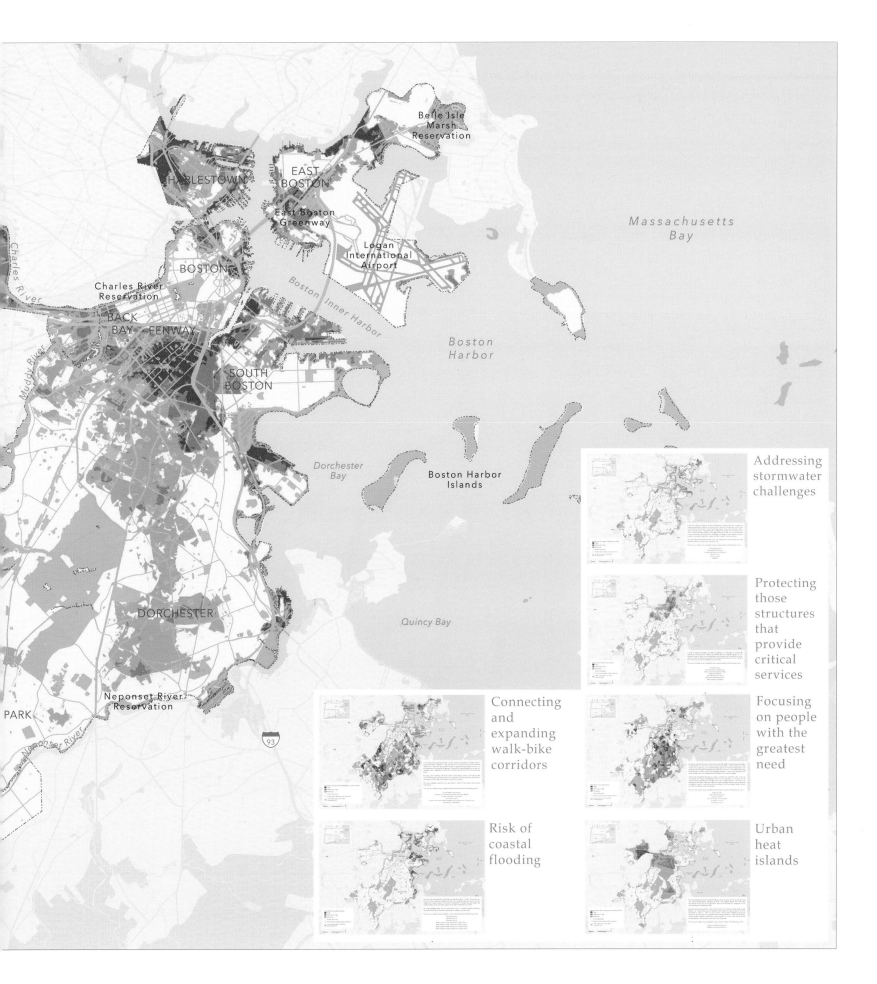

Belle Isle Marsh Reservation

EAST BOSTON

East Boston Greenway

Logan International Airport

CHARLESTOWN

BOSTON

Charles River Reservation

BACK BAY · FENWAY

Charles River

Muddy River

SOUTH BOSTON

Boston Inner Harbor

Massachusetts Bay

Boston Harbor

Boston Harbor Islands

Dorchester Bay

DORCHESTER

Quincy Bay

Neponset River Reservation

PARK

Neponset River

93

Addressing stormwater challenges

Protecting those structures that provide critical services

Connecting and expanding walk-bike corridors

Focusing on people with the greatest need

Risk of coastal flooding

Urban heat islands

SMART GEOPLANNER

Abu Dhabi Urban Planning Council
Abu Dhabi, United Arab Emirates
By Abu Dhabi Urban Planning Council

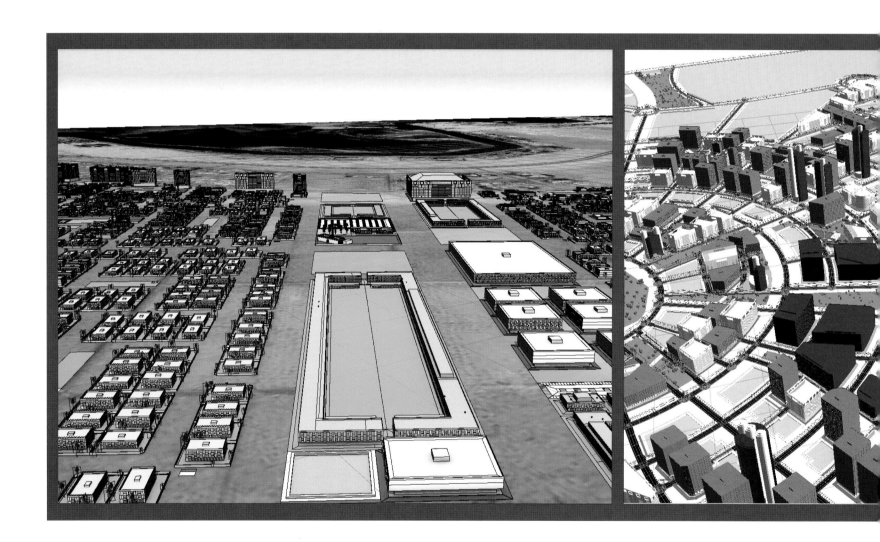

The Smart GeoPlanner System is an interactive map that facilitates access to the latest spatial data for the Abu Dhabi Department of Urban Planning and Municipalities. The system provides planners with smart tools that allow them to perform advance spatial analysis to support informed planning decisions. The system has been hailed as the flagship enterprise GIS system used from the executive management down to individual planners on a daily basis. The 3D visualization portal component of the system to compare current and future masterplans has been integrated into the system using Esri® CityEngine®

Courtesy of Abu Dhabi Urban Planning Council.

CONTACT
Samer Atiya
satiya@gmail.com

SOFTWARE
ArcGIS Desktop

DATA SOURCE
Abu Dhabi Urban Planning Council

3D NATIONAL MAP OF SINGAPORE

Singapore Land Authority
Singapore, Singapore
By Singapore Land Authority

Reality and thematic visualization of the 3D city models.

In 2014, the Singapore Land Authority (SLA) led a government initiative to create and maintain an authoritative 3D map of the entire country. The initiative involved capturing 3D data using aerial imaging and laser-scanning technologies. The project produced high-quality 3D city models which included terrain, buildings, and other infrastructure based on the OGC CityGML standard. These 3D datasets are shared with government agencies for applications in areas of operation, planning, risk management, and policy formulation.

Apart from the 3D topographic features above ground, SLA also completed the 3D modelling of subterranean ownership parcels from existing 2D cadastral survey plans. This 3D underground ownership is an essential dataset to support underground planning in Singapore.

Marina Bay area showing the integration of above ground 3D city models and underground ownership parcels.

CONTACT
Tong Wee Aw
aw_tong_wee@sla.gov.sg

SOFTWARE
ArcGIS Pro

DATA SOURCE
Singapore Land Authority

3D VISUALIZATION OF QUEEN STREET AND RAILWAY STREET 2019

Helsingborg City
Helsingborg, Skåne, Sweden
By Cleber Domingos Arruda

This image shows geodesign and visual simulation of a proposed street renovation in Helsingborg, Sweden. Helsingborg is growing fast which requires more things to coexist in the same space and increases demands on the infrastructure of the city center.

Therefore, city officials are developing Helsingborg's main thoroughfares, Queen Street and Railway Street, with better and more walking and cycling routes and places where people thrive and want to be. Public transport is a priority and the street will be part of the

Courtesy of Cleber Domingos Arruda. Copyright © 2017 Helsingborg City.

HelsingborgExpressen route in 2019 with two years of construction limiting accessibility. This 3D image shows residents how the project will look upon completion and is used on the city's website, in social media, and in meetings with different stakeholders.

CONTACT
Cleber Domingos Arruda
cleber.arruda@helsingborg.se

SOFTWARE
ArcGIS Pro,
Esri CityEngine

DATA SOURCE
Helsingborg City

ELECTRONIC MAP FOR LAND-USE PLANNING IN TYROL

Administration of the Tyrol
Innsbruck, Tyrol, Austria
By Andrea Jakob and tiris-Team

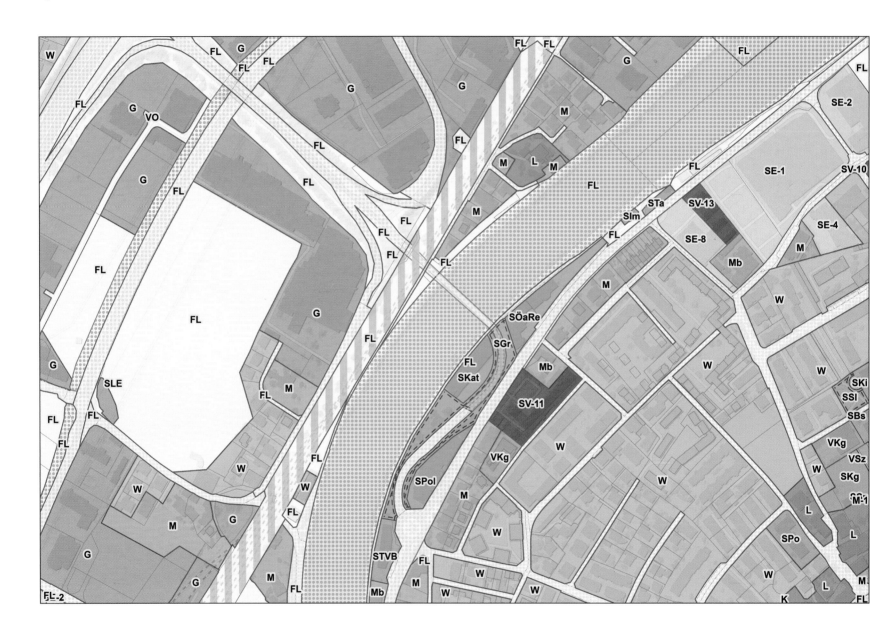

In accordance with the Tyrolean Spatial Planning Law, each municipality defines a land-use plan for the entire municipal area and keeps it up-to-date. Since 2013, the legal procedure for the approval of planning zones has been carried out electronically. Opinions, statements, declarations, decisions of the municipal council, and fixed periods and deadlines are registered in the system. This ensures that the entire workflow is processed and implemented according to legal requirements.

GIS plays a central role in building up the land-use plan first by importing geodata into the electronic system and with ongoing support throughout all planning stages. Geoprocessing routines ensure the fully automated and fast production of legally binding plans.

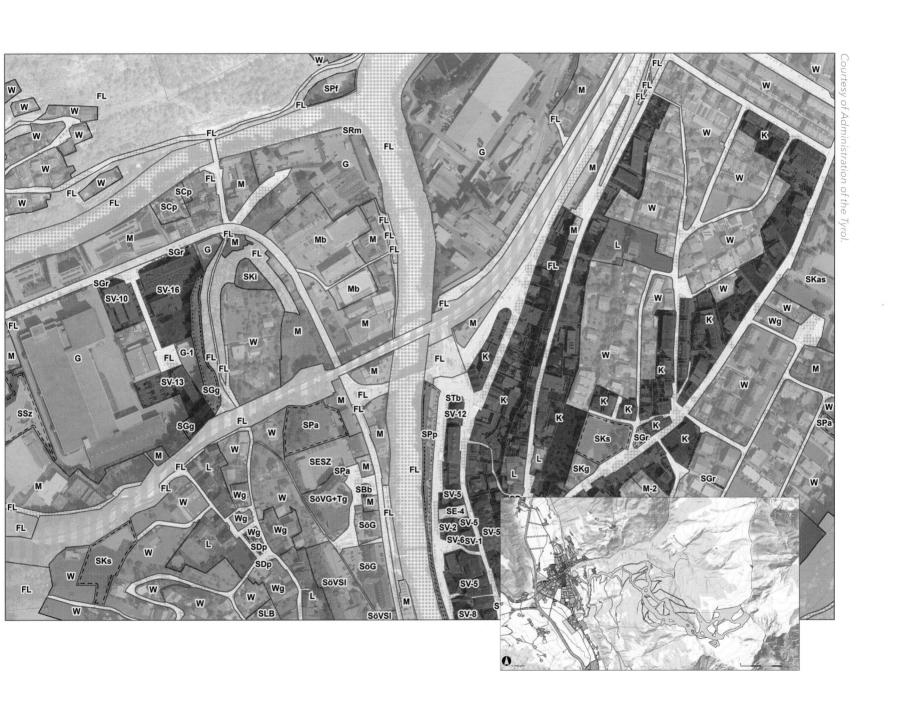

CONTACT
Johann Niedertscheider
landesstatistik.tiris@tirol.gv.at

SOFTWARE
ArcGIS Server 10.4,
Synergis WebOffice 10.5

DATA SOURCE
tiris (GIS Tyrol)

TRACKING THE SHARE OF IOT

This map features highlights from ShareTracker's recent study of the Internet of Things (IoT) across the United States. In this view, sensors were discovered for 138,000 devices in the Hampton Roads, Virginia, area. These devices captured data from a wide variety of categories, including personal computers, tablets, mobile phones, home security systems, gaming consoles, smart home appliances, smart speakers, televisions, and video devices. This analysis provides a geospatial reference for broadband service providers and consumers to see how and where technology is evolving.

ShareTracker, LLC
Ashland, Missouri, USA
By Mark Amato and Michelle Doyle

CONTACT
Michelle Doyle
MDoyle@ShareTracker.net

SOFTWARE
ArcGIS Pro 1.4

DATA SOURCE
ShareTracker, LLC

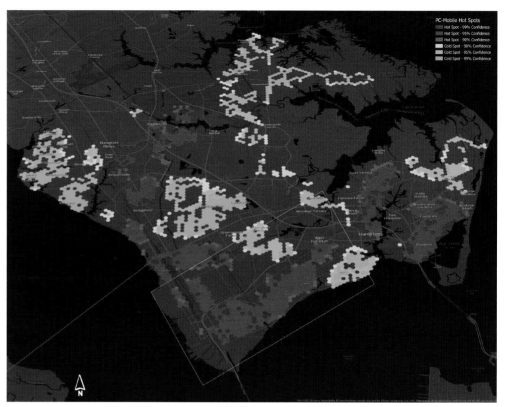

Highlights of ShareTracker's recent study of IoT across the USA. These maps portray IoT concentrations for the most popular brands within 'PCs-Mobile Data' and 'Video Data' featured segments studied within the Hampton Roads, VA market in March 2017.

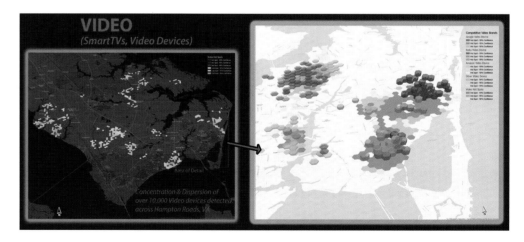

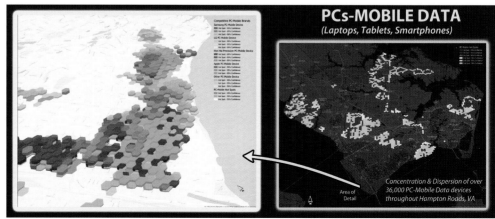

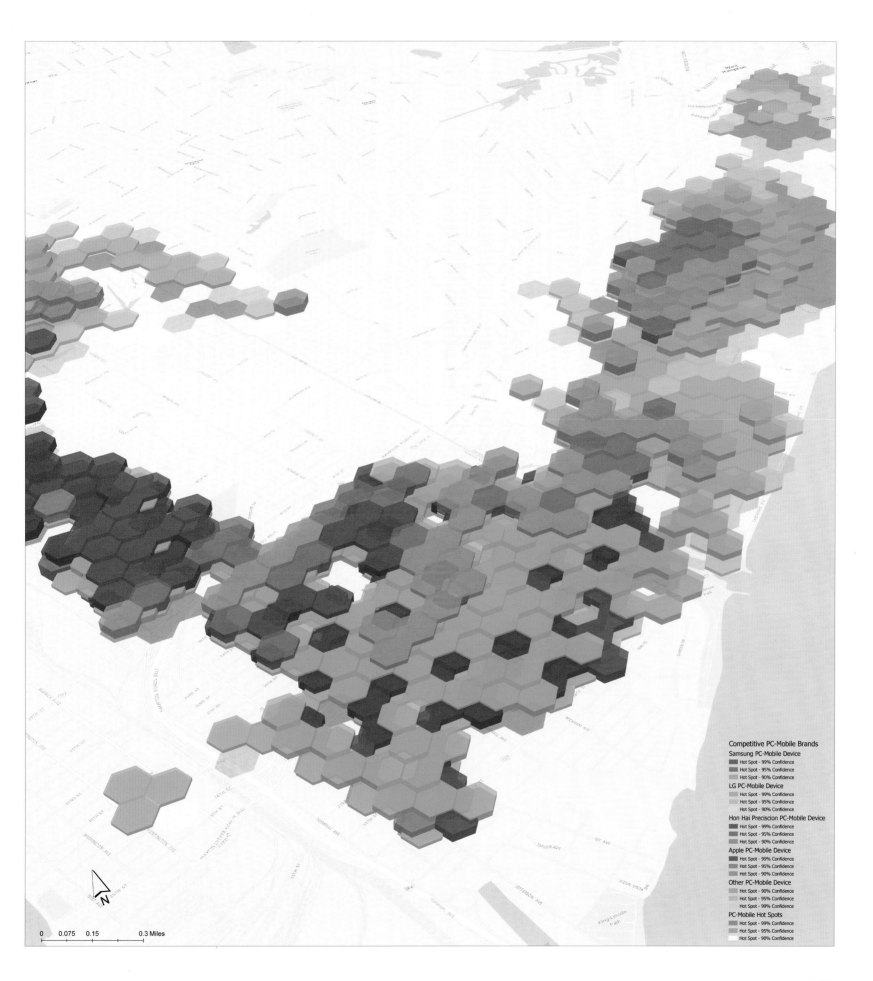

Competitive PC-Mobile Brands

Samsung PC-Mobile Device
Hot Spot - 99% Confidence
Hot Spot - 95% Confidence
Hot Spot - 90% Confidence

LG PC-Mobile Device
Hot Spot - 99% Confidence
Hot Spot - 95% Confidence
Hot Spot - 90% Confidence

Hon Hai Precision PC-Mobile Device
Hot Spot - 99% Confidence
Hot Spot - 95% Confidence
Hot Spot - 90% Confidence

Apple PC-Mobile Device
Hot Spot - 99% Confidence
Hot Spot - 95% Confidence
Hot Spot - 90% Confidence

Other PC-Mobile Device
Hot Spot - 90% Confidence
Hot Spot - 95% Confidence
Hot Spot - 99% Confidence

PC-Mobile Hot Spots
Hot Spot - 99% Confidence
Hot Spot - 95% Confidence
Hot Spot - 90% Confidence

0   0.075   0.15   0.3 Miles

CELLULAR COVERAGE MODELING IN THE UNITED KINGDOM

Cellular Expert Company
Vilnius, Lithuania
By Vytautas Ramonaitis and Svajunas Vitkauskas

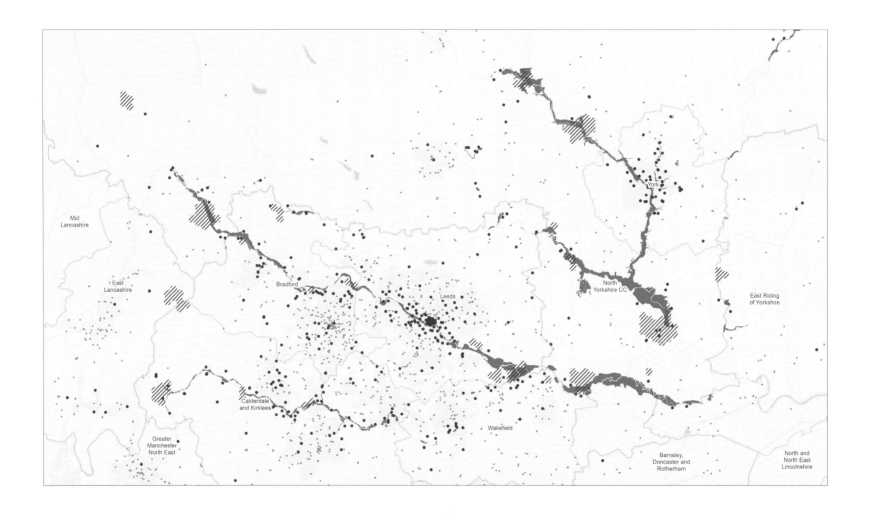

This series of images shows the analysis by Cellular Expert Company of flood impacts to the 4G communication network during the flooding in Yorkshire, United Kingdom, which occurred on December 26, 2015. A dedicated app for ArcGIS Portal/Online shows the network parameters: availability, area of limited connectivity and number of faults during different periods. Floodwaters from rivers Aire, Ouse, and Foss caused damage to mobile network infrastructure disconnecting some base stations from the network.

The analysis of wireless network connectivity for first responders in flood-affected areas is based on satellite-derived data. Wireless sites damaged by flooding are shown as red dots. The rest of mobile base stations shown in green continue to operate but with reduced cellular network coverage. The areas with insufficient signal quality are marked by red stripes. As the number of flood-affected sites increased, the areas with limited connectivity also increased in size. The connectivity is influenced not only by reduced coverage, but also by traffic overload when rescue teams must access a limited number of remaining base stations.

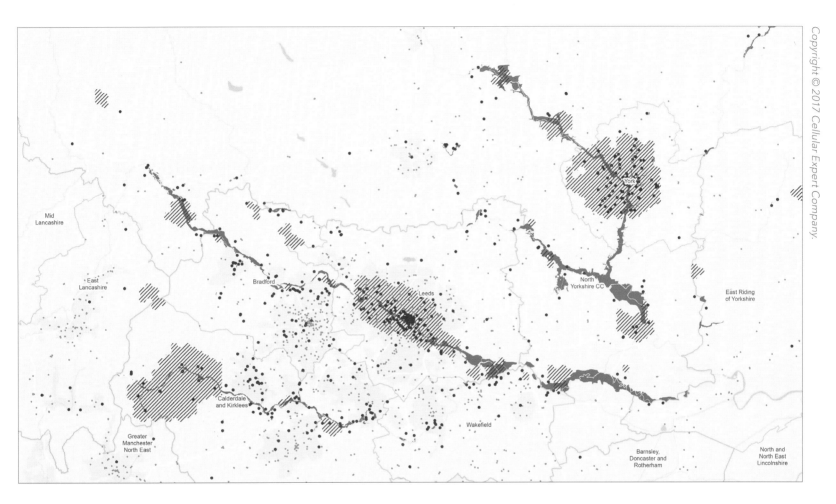

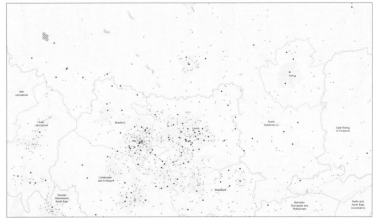

CONTACT
Viktorija Rynkeviciute
VRynkeviciute@cellular-expert.com

SOFTWARE
Operations Dashboard for ArcGIS®

DATA SOURCE
Cellular Expert Company

CALIFORNIA–NEVADA TOURIST MAP

This map of California and Nevada is part of the Michelin's product range, including tour guides, road maps, city maps, and atlases, and provides up-to-date and reliable information for travelers. Michelin has designed and produced maps since 1910, and covers seventy countries in the world at various scales.

Michelin Travel Partner
Boulogne-Billancourt, France
By Cartography Team,
Michelin Travel Partner

CONTACT
Philippe Sablayrolles
psablayrolles@tp.michelin.com

SOFTWARE
ArcGIS Desktop 10.2

DATA SOURCE
Michelin Travel Partner

WASATCH FRONT RECREATION

A portion of the Wasatch Front extending from Provo Canyon to Parleys Canyon is a high-use area of the Uinta-Wasatch-Cache National Forest. This portion of the forest shares direct proximity to Salt Lake City and other neighboring cities. This provides direct access to more than one million people living along the boundary of the national forest. This map shows a variety of recreational opportunities available. Camping, hiking, picnicking, and skiing are just some of the many activates. The Uinta-Wasatch-Cache National Forest is considered one of the urban national forests in the Forest Service system and covers an area that includes northern Utah and a small portion of southwest Wyoming.

US Department of Agriculture (USDA)
Forest Service
Salt Lake City, Utah, USA
By Andrew Keske

CONTACT
Andrew Keske
akeske@fs.fed.us

SOFTWARE
ArcGIS Desktop 10.3.1, Natural Scenes Designer Pro 5.0, Adobe Photoshop CC 2015.5, Adobe Illustrator CC 2015.3

DATA SOURCES
USDA Forest Service and US Geological Survey

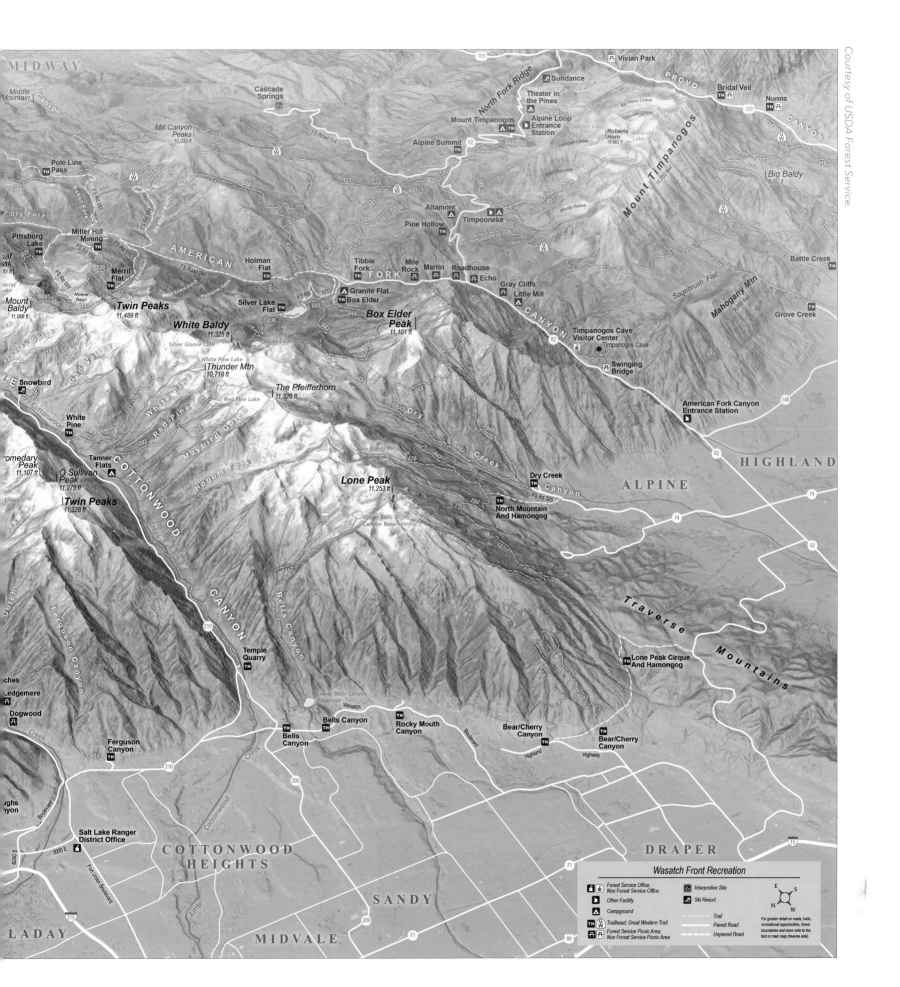

MIDWAY

Middle
Mountain

Mill Canyon
Peaks
10,335 ft

Cascade
Springs

North Fork Ridge

Vivian Park

Sundance

Theater in
the Pines

Mount Timpanogos

Alpine Loop
Entrance
Station

Bridal Veil

Nunns

PROVO CANYON

Pole Line
Pass

Alpine Summit

Altamont

Pine Hollow

Timpooneke

Mount Timpanogos
11,752 ft

Big Baldy
9,751 ft

Miller Hill
Mining

AMERICAN

FORK

Merril
Flat

Twin Peaks
11,489 ft

Holman
Flat

Silver Lake
Flat

Tibble
Fork

Mile
Rock

Martin

Roadhouse

Echo

CANYON

Battle Creek

Mahogany Mtn
9,008 feet

Sagebrush Flat

Grove Creek

Pittsburg
Lake

Dry Fork

Mount
Baldy
11,068 ft

White Baldy
11,325 ft

Box Elder
Peak
11,101 ft

Granite Flat
Box Elder

Gray Cliffs
Little Mill

Thunder Mtn
10,718 ft

Silver Glance Lake

Silver Lake

White Pine Lake

The Pfeifferhorn
11,326 ft

Timpanogos Cave
Visitor Center

Timpanogos Cave

Snowbird

White
Pine

Red Pine Lake

Red Pine

Maybird Gulch

Hogum Fork

Dry

Creek

Swinging
Bridge

American Fork Canyon
Entrance Station

146

Dromedary
Peak
11,107 ft

Tanner
Flats

O Sullivan
Peak
11,275 ft

Lake Hardy

Lone Peak
11,253 ft

Dry Creek
Canyon

FS Rd 325

North Mountain
And Hamongog

HIGHLAND

ALPINE

74

Twin Peaks
11,328 ft

COTTONWOOD

Upper Bells
Canyon Reservoir

92

Ferguson Canyon

CANYON

Bells Canyon

Temple
Quarry

Lower Bells Canyon
Reservoir

Wasatch

Bells Canyon

Rocky Mouth
Canyon

Bear/Cherry
Canyon

Bear/Cherry
Canyon

Traverse

Lone Peak Cirque
And Hamongog

Mountains

210

Boulevard

Highland

Highway

Ferguson
Canyon

Dogwood

Ledgemere

Salt Lake Ranger
District Office

COTTONWOOD
HEIGHTS

209

Cottonwood

Creek

DRAPER

I-15

6200 S

3000 E

SANDY

15

LADAY

MIDVALE

209

71

89

Wasatch Front Recreation

Forest Service Office; Non Forest Service Office	Interpretive Site	
Other Facility	Ski Resort	
Campground		
Trailhead; Great Western Trail	Trail	
Forest Service Picnic Area; Non Forest Service Picnic Area	Paved Road	
	Unpaved Road	

For greater detail on roads, trails,
recreational opportunities, forest
boundaries and more refer to the
text or main map (reverse side).

BARANOF ISLAND, TONGASS NATIONAL FOREST

These maps highlight the recreational opportunities available on the Sitka Ranger District of the Tongass National Forest on Baranof Island. Baranof Island is one of the larger temperate rain-forest Islands of the Alexander Archipelago located in the Inland Passage of southeastern Alaska. At 1,607 square miles, it is the tenth largest island in the United States and boasts 617 miles of shoreline. The maps locate the island's campgrounds, picnic areas, trailheads, boat launching ramps, and swimming areas.

US Department of Agriculture (USDA)
Forest Service
Juneau, Alaska, USA
By Robert Francis, Dustin Wittwer,
 Andrew Keske, Matthew Tharp, Jesse Nett,
Kevin Kolb and Faith Duncan.

CONTACT
Robert Francis
rfrancis@fs.fed.us

SOFTWARE
ArcGIS Desktop 10.3,
Adobe Illustrator

DATA SOURCE
USDA Forest Service

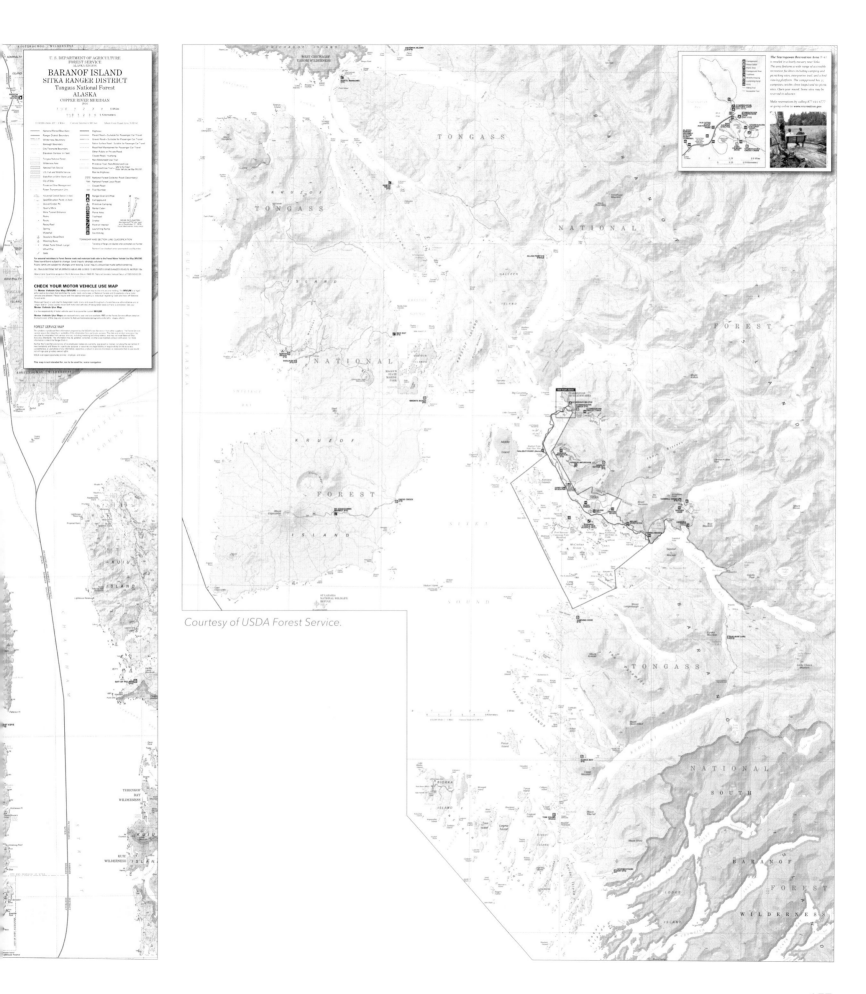

Courtesy of USDA Forest Service.

TRANSIT AUTHORITY OF NORTHERN KENTUCKY

Public transportation in Kenton County is provided by the Transit Authority of Northern Kentucky (TANK). TANK is part of the regional transit system that serves Northern Kentucky and Southwest Ohio (via Metro north of the Ohio River). TANK operates eight local routes including the Southbank Shuttle, five express routes, and seven park and ride locations in Kenton County. This map charts public transportation ridership and gas cost for various routes of the system.

Planning and Development Services (PDS) of Kenton County Fort Mitchell, Kentucky, USA
By Louis Hill, Ryan Kent, and Trisha Brush

CONTACT
Ryan Hermann
rhermann@pdskc.org

SOFTWARE
ArcGIS Desktop 10.4,
CorelDRAW x7

DATA SOURCES
PDS of Kenton County, LINK-GIS, Transit Authority of Northern Kentucky (TANK)

Southbank Trolley
(Busses prohibited
on Roebling Bridge)

Rt 3 - Ludlow Bromley: Ridership & Gas Cost

Rt 1 - Florence: Ridership & Gas Cost

Rt 7 - Rosedale Latonia: Ridership & Gas Cost

Rt 25 - Alexandria Eastern: Ridership & Gas Cost

Rt 24 - NKU Shuttle: Ridership & Gas Cost

Rt 33 - St Elizabeth / Edgewood: Ridership & Gas Cost

Main TANK Garage
and Fort Wright Hub

35X East-West Express
"Ride 35" added in 2014

Daniel Carter Beard Bridge

Brent Spence Bridge

Clay Wade Bailey Bridge

Roebling Bridge

Taylor Southgate Bridge

Ohio River

Little Miami River

Licking River

MERRILL FIELD AIRPORT MASTER PLAN UPDATE AND NOISE EXPOSURE PLAN

HDR Alaska, Inc.
San Diego, California, USA
By Vanessa Bauman

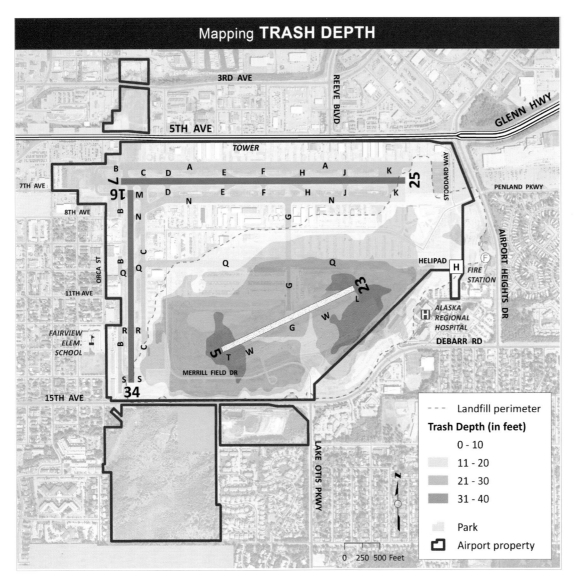

Mapping **TRASH DEPTH**

- - - Landfill perimeter
Trash Depth (in feet)
0 - 10
11 - 20
21 - 30
31 - 40

Park
Airport property

0 250 500 Feet

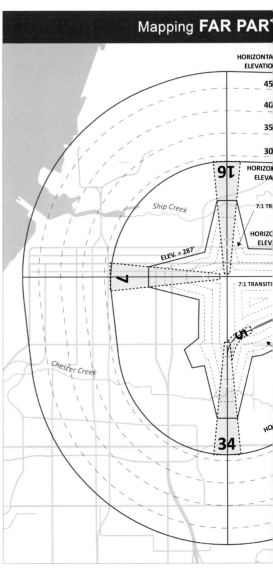

Mapping **FAR PART**

The Municipality of Anchorage contracted with HDR to provide airport planning and engineering services in developing a master plan update for Merrill Field Airport. In phase 1 of this update, HDR compiled GIS data collected during the existing inventory assessment and supported a data gap analysis. This information was incorporated with additional survey data collected for the master plan update in phase 2 of the project and integrated into the FAA Airports GIS system.

In phase 2 of the project, HDR was responsible for eALP development and map production for the final airport master plan report. HDR also conducted airport planning research and created maps and graphics for public involvement activities.

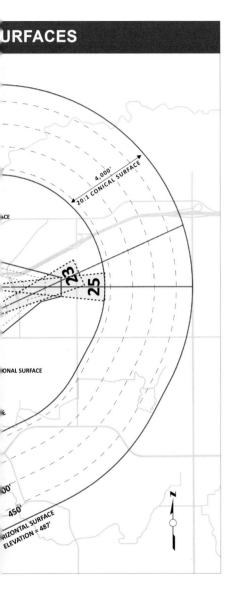

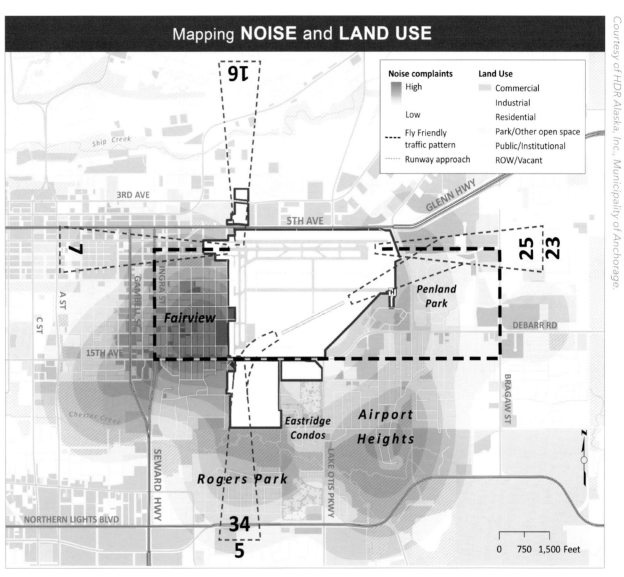

Mapping **NOISE** and **LAND USE**

Noise complaints
- High
- Low
- - - Fly Friendly traffic pattern
- ⋯ Runway approach

Land Use
- Commercial
- Industrial
- Residential
- Park/Other open space
- Public/Institutional
- ROW/Vacant

Ship Creek

3RD AVE

5TH AVE

GLENN HWY

7

16

25
23

A ST

C ST

GAMBELL ST

INGRA ST

SEWARD HWY

Fairview

15TH AVE

Penland Park

DEBARR RD

Chester Creek

Eastridge Condos

Airport Heights

BRAGAW ST

LAKE OTIS PKWY

Rogers Park

34
5

NORTHERN LIGHTS BLVD

0   750   1,500 Feet

Courtesy of HDR Alaska, Inc., Municipality of Anchorage.

CONTACT
Anders Burvall
anders.burvall@hdrinc.com

SOFTWARE
ArcGIS Desktop10.4

DATA SOURCE
HDR Alaska, Inc., Municipality of Anchorage

THE NORTHWEST SEAPORT ALLIANCE NORTH AND SOUTH HARBOR MAPS

The Northwest Seaport Alliance (NWSA) is a marine cargo operating partnership between the Port of Seattle and the Port of Tacoma. The cartographic responsibilities encompass the land area of each port, which are approximately 30 miles apart. These two maps are part of a larger marketing piece highlighting the port's facilities and services and include visuals for transload warehousing and cold storage facilities. Major routes in and out of the port, and the heavy haul corridor (a designated route for oversized cargo transportation) are also emphasized.

The goal of these maps is to show the location, size, and proximity to rails and roads of cargo terminals in a large-scale view, and are used by both external customers and internally as a land-use reference. The maps were created with data layers for water, roads/highways, rail, rail yards, port properties, NWSA properties, buildings, and hillshade.

The Northwest Seaport Alliance (NWSA)
Tacoma, Washington, USA
By Karen Zeeb

CONTACT
Karen Zeeb
kzeeb@nwseaportalliance.com

SOFTWARE
ArcGIS Desktop, ArcGIS Online,
Adobe Illustrator

DATA SOURCES
Port of Tacoma, Port of Seattle, Washington Department of Transportation,
City of Tacoma, City of Seattle, King County,
Pierce County

Courtesy of NWSA

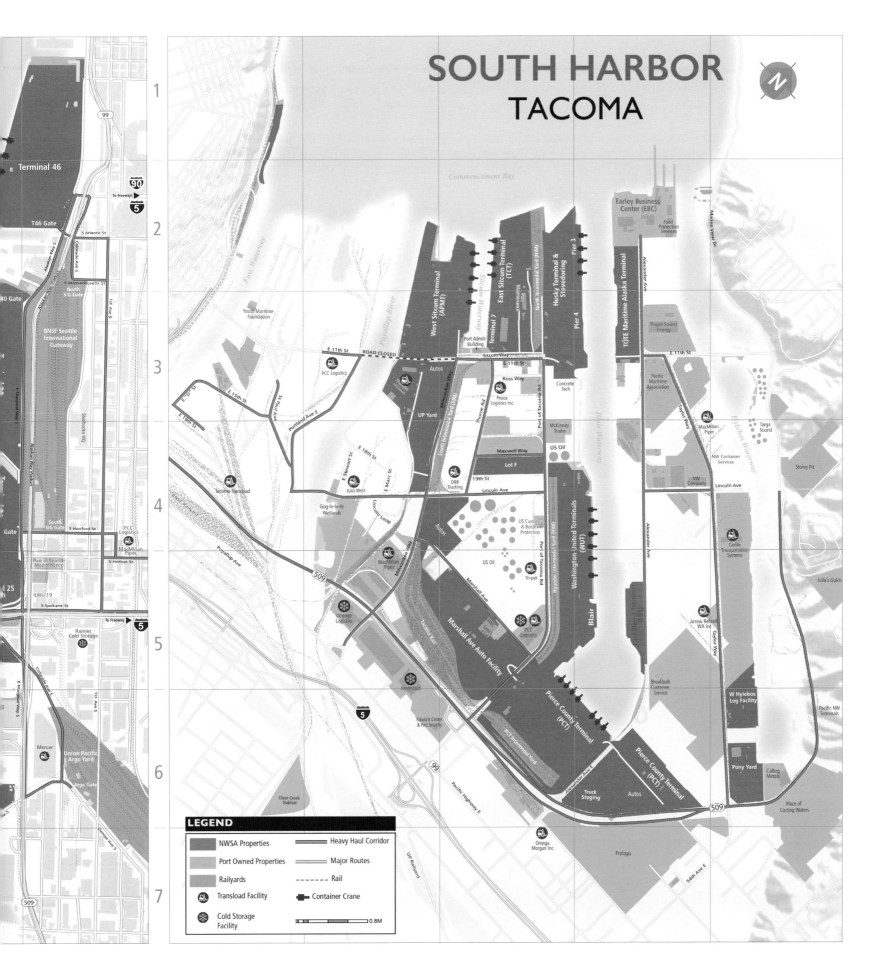

SOUTH HARBOR
TACOMA

Commencement Bay

Terminal 46

T46 Gate

S Atlantic St

North SIG Gate

S Massachusetts St

Colorado Ave S

1st Ave S

Alaskan Way S

BNSF Seattle International Gateway

Starbucks HQ

Youth Maritime Foundation

Puyallup River

East Waterway

West Sitcum Terminal (APMT)

East Sitcum Terminal (TCT)

Terminal 7

North Intermodal Yard (NIM)

Husky Terminal & Stevedoring (HTM)

Pier 3

Pier 4

Earley Business Center (EBC)

Food Protection Services

Maritime View Dr

TOTE Maritime Alaska Terminal

Alexander Ave

Puget Sound Energy

Port Admin Building

Sitcum Way

E 11th St

ROAD CLOSED

E 11th St

E 11th St

Sitcum Waterway

PCC Logistics

E 11th St

Autos

Milwaukee Way

Ross Way

Thorne Rd

Port of Tacoma Rd

Concrete Tech

Pacific Maritime Association

Taylor Way

MacMillan Piper

Targa Sound

E 15th St

St Paul Ave

Portland Ave E

South Intermodal Yard (SIM)

UP Yard

Peace Logistics Inc.

McKinney Trailer

US Oil

Blair Waterway

NW Container Services

Storey Pit

E 70 St

E 18th St

E Stewart St

E Marc St

Maxwell Way

Lot F

D&B Trucking

19th St

US Oil

Hyundai Intermodal Yard (HIM)

NW Company

Lincoln Ave

KAG West

Lincoln Ave

Tacoma Transload

Gog-le-hi-te Wetlands

Lincoln Loop

Autos

MacMillan Piper

US Customs & Border Protection

Washington United Terminals (WUT)

Carlile Transportation Systems

Julia's Gulch

BNSF Railyard

Puyallup Ave

509

Milwaukee Way

Tri-pak

US Oil

Port of Tacoma Rd

Marshall Ave

Alexander Ave

Arrow Reload WA Inc

Lineage Logistics

Tacoma Rail

PCC Logistics

Blair

Taylor Way

Marshall Ave Auto Facility

Pierce County Terminal (PCT)

Breakbulk Customer Service

W Hylebos Log Facility

Pacific NW Terminals

5

Americold

Fabulich Center & Port Security

99

Pacific Highway E

PCT Intermodal Yard

Alexander Ave E

Pierce County Terminal (PCT)

Truck Staging

Autos

Pony Yard

Calbag Metals

Place of Circling Waters

Clear Creek Habitat

UP Railyard

Omega Morgan Inc

Prologis

Truck Staging

509

54th Ave E

509

LEGEND

	NWSA Properties		Heavy Haul Corridor
	Port Owned Properties		Major Routes
	Railyards	- - - -	Rail
	Transload Facility		Container Crane
	Cold Storage Facility		0.8M

IMPACT OF THE METRORAIL

Houston light rail transit (METRORail) is operated by the Metropolitan Transit Authority of Harris County. It opened to the public in January 2004. The transit system provides commuters and the transit-dependent population with better access to economic opportunities and social activities.

This study of METRORail data reveals the impact of the system on property values in Houston with a 1-mile buffer. It employs property value increases, no change, and decreases to identify the effects. From this study, METRORail has been found to generate significant increases in commercial and residential property values.

Harris County Appraisal District (HCAD)
Houston, Texas, USA
By Michael Vy and Linghui "Nina" Zeng

CONTACT
Linghui Zeng
Lzeng@hcad.org

SOFTWARE
ArcGIS Desktop 10.5

DATA SOURCE
HCAD

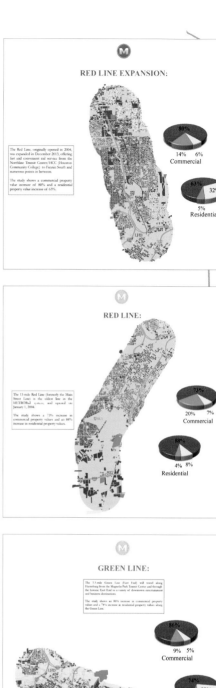

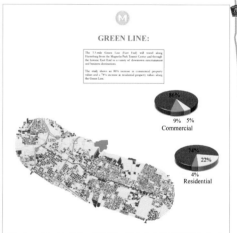

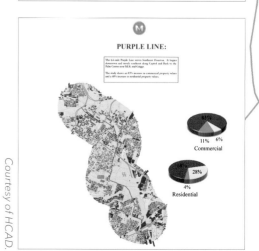

Courtesy of HCAD.

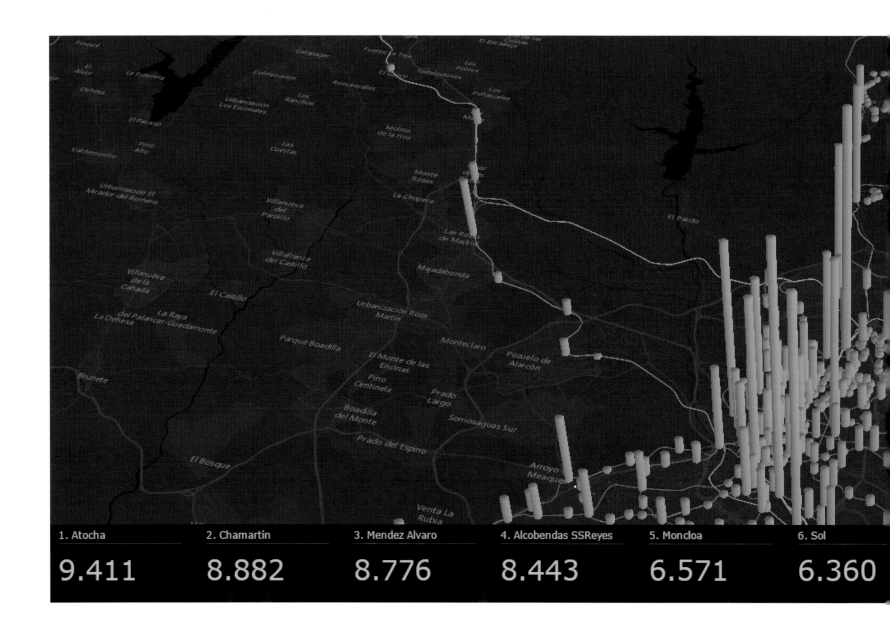

1. Atocha	2. Chamartin	3. Mendez Alvaro	4. Alcobendas SSReyes	5. Moncloa	6. Sol
9.411	8.882	8.776	8.443	6.571	6.360

3D APPLICATION OF THE BIG DATA STUDY

Consorcio Regional de Transportes de Madrid (Regional Transport Consortium of Madrid) Madrid, Madrid, Spain By Alicia Hernández Luengo

The Regional Transport Consortium of Madrid was formed in 1985 to coordinate public transportation operations across multiple rail and bus providers in Madrid, Spain. The integration of planning tasks and coordination of infrastructure, services, and fare policy results in efficient and quality transit service for its customers.

This 3D app shows the results of the consortium's big data study examining the evolution of demand in public transport during the suspension of service on Line 8 of the Metro Network. It allows for the visualization of the demand for all public transport users or for the habitual Line 8 users. It also allows for the visualization of the difference of validations in stops per day with respect

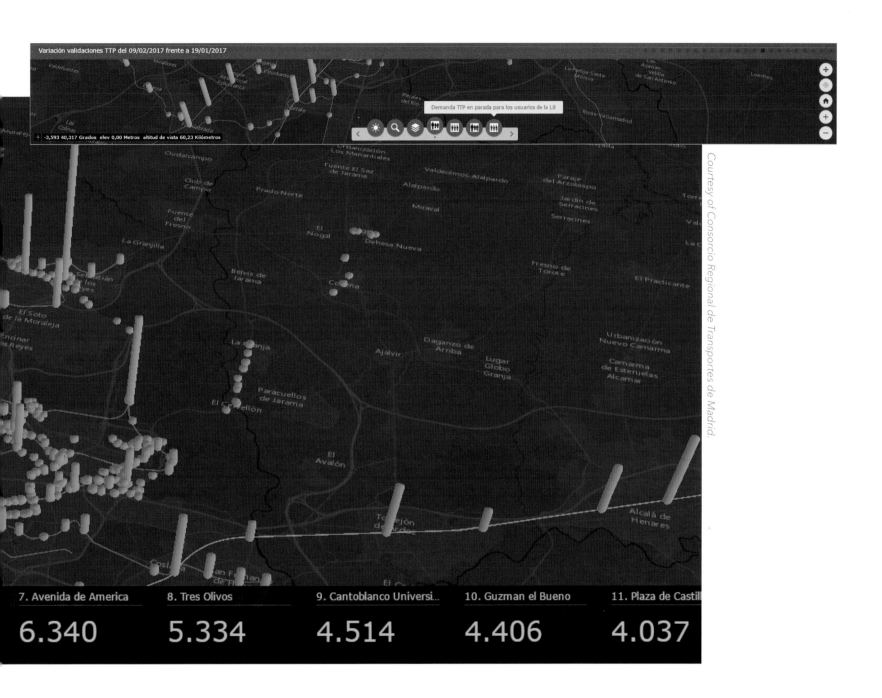

Variación validaciones TTP del 09/02/2017 frente a 19/01/2017

Demanda TTP en parada para los usuarios de la L8

-3,593 40,317 Grados elev 0,00 Metros altitud de vista 60,23 Kilómetros

7. Avenida de America	8. Tres Olivos	9. Cantoblanco Universi...	10. Guzman el Bueno	11. Plaza de Castill...
6.340	5.334	4.514	4.406	4.037

to the same day of a generic week previous to the suspension of Line 8 service for all users or habitual Line 8 users. This analysis was carried out during the entire time Line 8 was suspended and the app was used exclusively by workers within the Regional Transport Consortium.

CONTACT
Alicia Hernández Luengo
alicia.hernandez@crtm.es

SOFTWARE
ArcGIS Desktop,
ArcGIS Server,
ArcGIS Online,
Open Data

DATA SOURCE
Consorcio Regional de
Transportes de Madrid

NORTH AMERICAN NATURAL GAS SYSTEM

The last five years of gas pipeline development have been among the most active in US gas market history because of the growth of shale gas production, particularly in the Appalachian Basin in the northeast region. This expansion continues with many projects built to move Marcellus and Utica shale gas deeper into the premium gas markets along the East Coast and into other regions, including the Southeast where gas is now exported in liquefied form to international markets. Growing demand in Mexico has also prompted large expansions south across the border.

The North American Natural Gas System wall map reflects these developments as it continues to set the industry standard for visualizing the supply, generation, distribution, and transportation of natural gas across North America. This benchmark map will help viewers stay current on an evolving industry with the latest proposed pipeline products, proposed generation projects, storage, and more.

S&P Global Platts
Denver, Colorado, USA
By Ginny Mason

CONTACT
Ginny Mason
ginny.mason@spglobal.com

SOFTWARE
ArcGIS® Desktop 10.3 Standard,
Adobe Illustrator CS6, Avenza MAPublisher

DATA SOURCE
S&P Global Platts

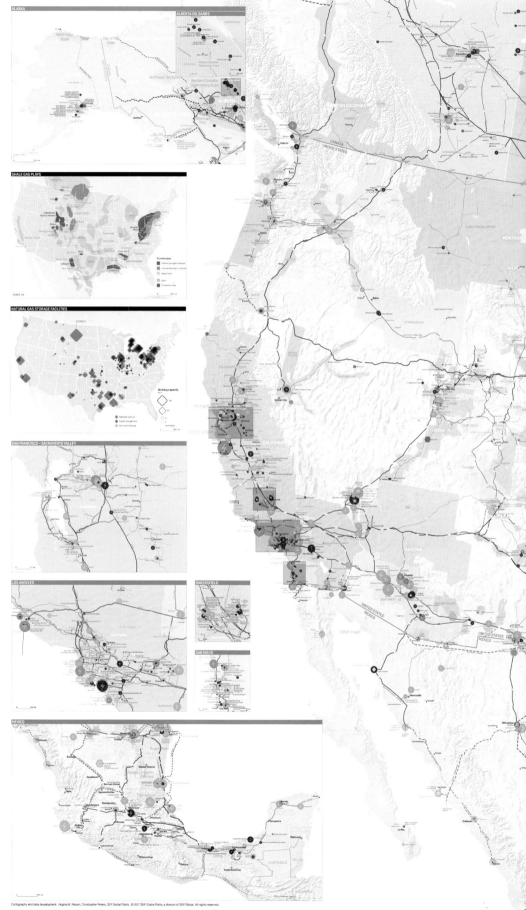

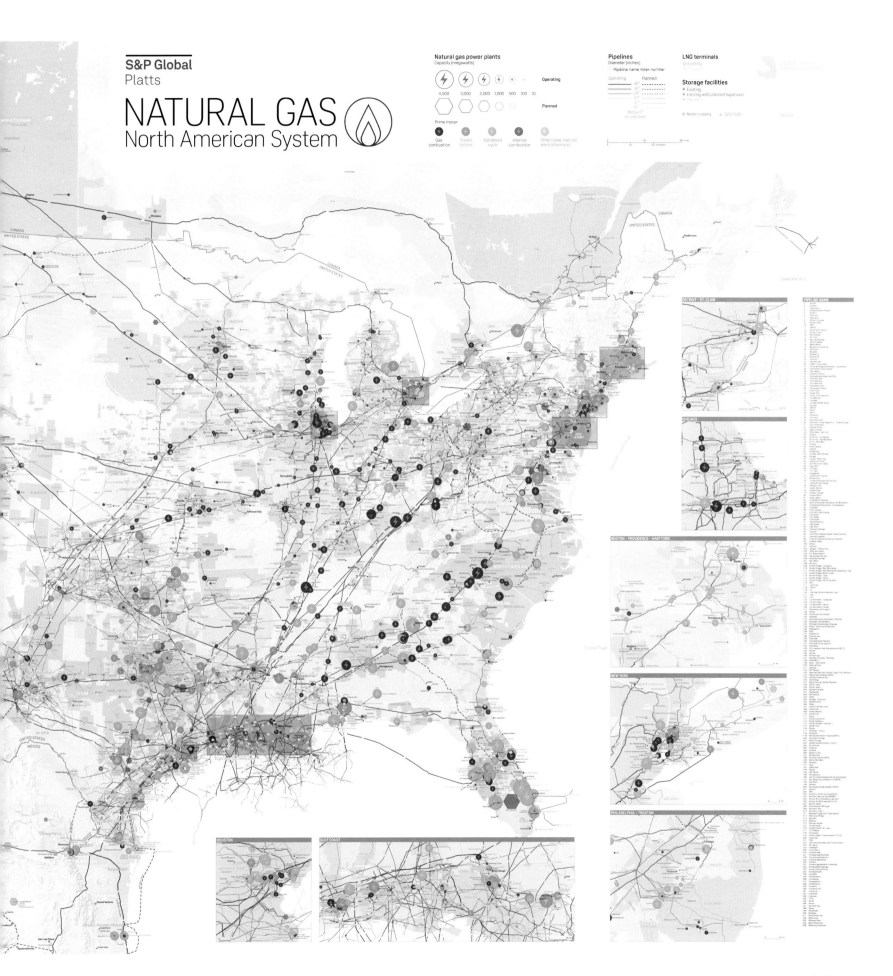

NATURAL GAS
North American System

S&P Global Platts

PLANNED GENERATION IN NORTH AMERICA

This map highlights the changing power generation fuel mix in the United States. The increased generation from renewable energy sources, such as wind and solar, take prominence in areas formerly dominated by coal and natural gas. Natural gas in the United States still dominates recent generation outputs, but may see higher gas fuel costs, particularly in Texas regions. This could bring existing coal plants back into the generation stack in coal-generating regions.

Maps showing the spatial distribution of power generation document the regional influence fuel costs and consumer trends have on the changing landscape.

S&P Global Platts
Denver, Colorado, USA
By Ginny Mason

CONTACT
Ginny Mason
ginny.mason@spglobal.com

SOFTWARE
ArcGIS Desktop 10.3 Standard,
Adobe products, Avenza MAPublisher

DATA SOURCE
S&P Global Platts

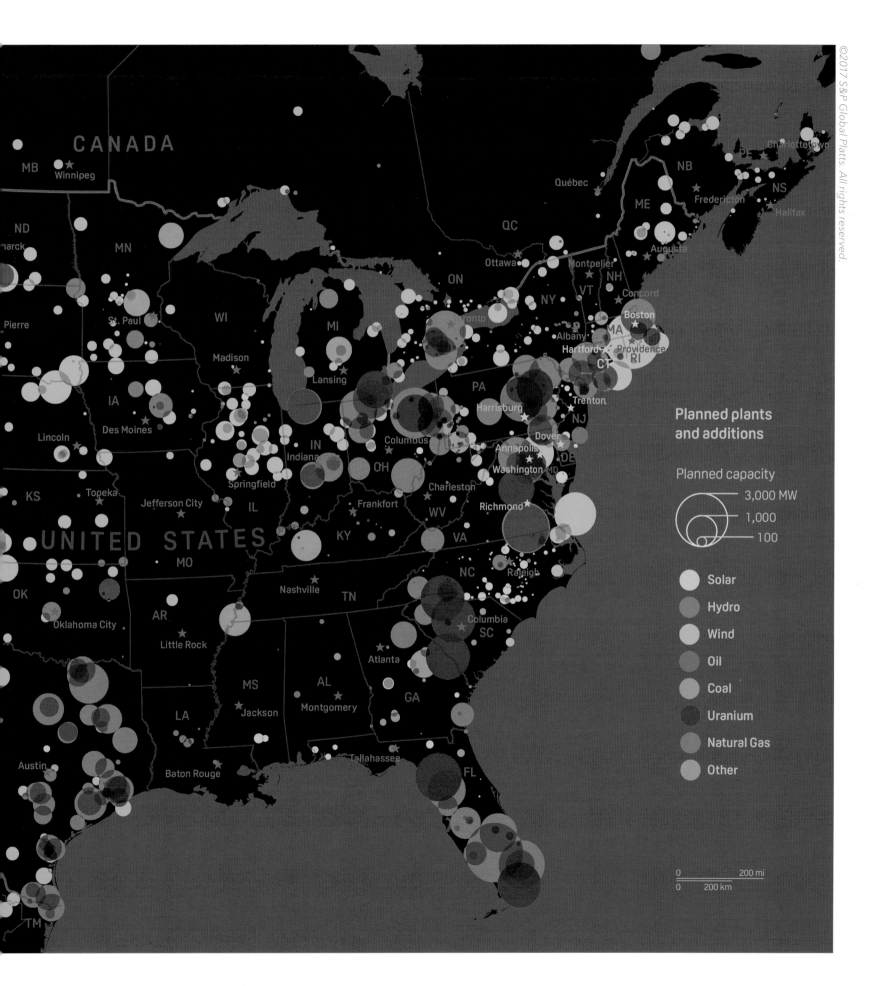

Planned plants and additions

Planned capacity

3,000 MW
1,000
100

- Solar
- Hydro
- Wind
- Oil
- Coal
- Uranium
- Natural Gas
- Other

0   200 mi
0   200 km

WEST BASIN MUNICIPAL WATER DISTRICT'S RECYCLED WATER USAGE VOLUMES

The West Basin Municipal Water District supplies more than 170,000 acre-feet of purified recycled waters annually to seventeen cities and unincorporated areas in Los Angeles County. West Basin operates a treatment facility that produces 40 million gallons of reusable water every day that meets the needs of municipal, commercial, and industrial customers. West Basin also supplies about 10 percent of the recycled waters annually to barrier injection wells along the Los Angeles County's coastline to prevent seawater intrusion to the groundwater.

This figure displays the district's 2016 recycled water usage volumes in Los Angeles County. It helps West Basin staff to understand where the large volumes of recycled waters are being consumed and to plan better management of pipelines.

West Basin Municipal Water District
Carson, California, USA
By Jinho Kang, GISP

CONTACT
Jinho Kang
jinho.kang@outlook.com

SOFTWARE
ArcGIS Desktop 10.5

DATA SOURCE
West Basin Municipal Water District

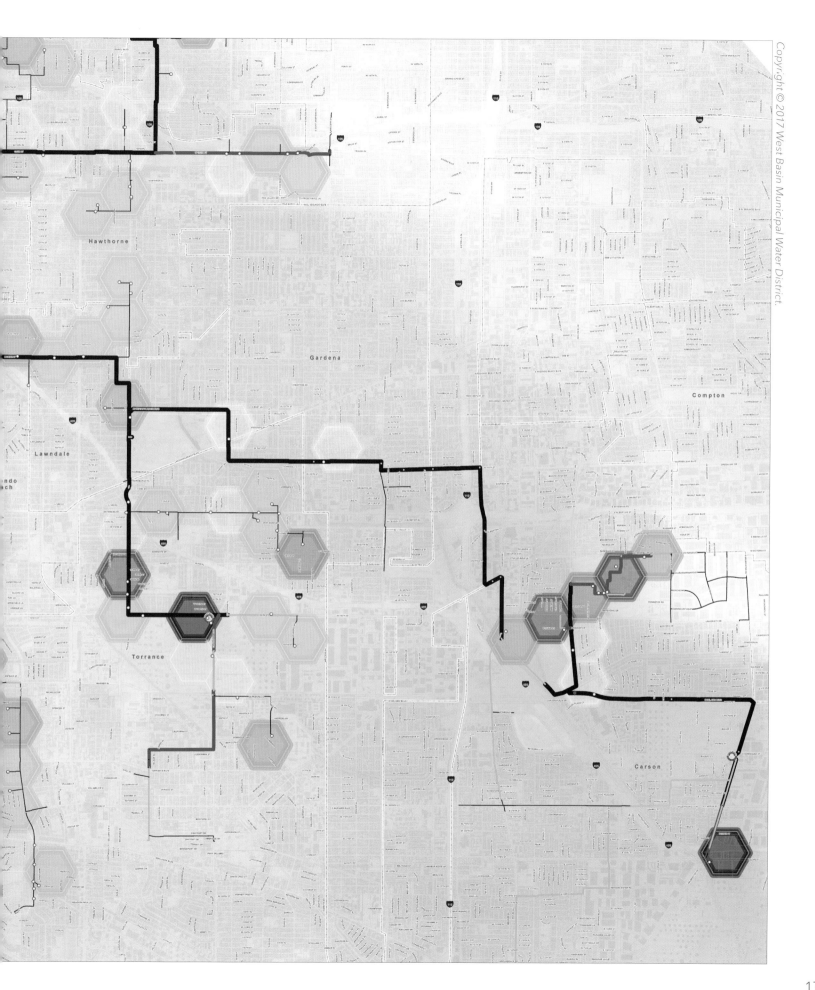

COBB COUNTY SEWER FACILITIES

The Cobb County Water System collects sewage from over 150,000 customers over more than 2,500 miles of gravity mains. The infrastructure used to collect this massive amount of wastewater is mapped in an enterprise GIS system using a variety of sources including as-builts, GPS, final plats, and various field data. This data is made available to the public as a 111-page map book for planning purposes and general usage, such as residential and commercial connections as well as commercial planning.

Cobb County Water System
Marietta, Georgia, USA
By James Primm

CONTACT
Matthew Johnson
matthew.johnson@cobbcounty.org

SOFTWARE
ArcGIS Desktop 10.3.1,
Adobe Photoshop CC 2017

DATA SOURCE
Cobb County Water System

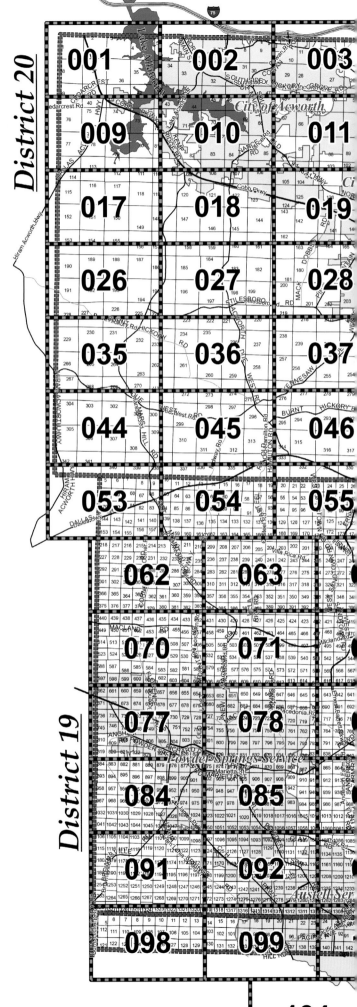

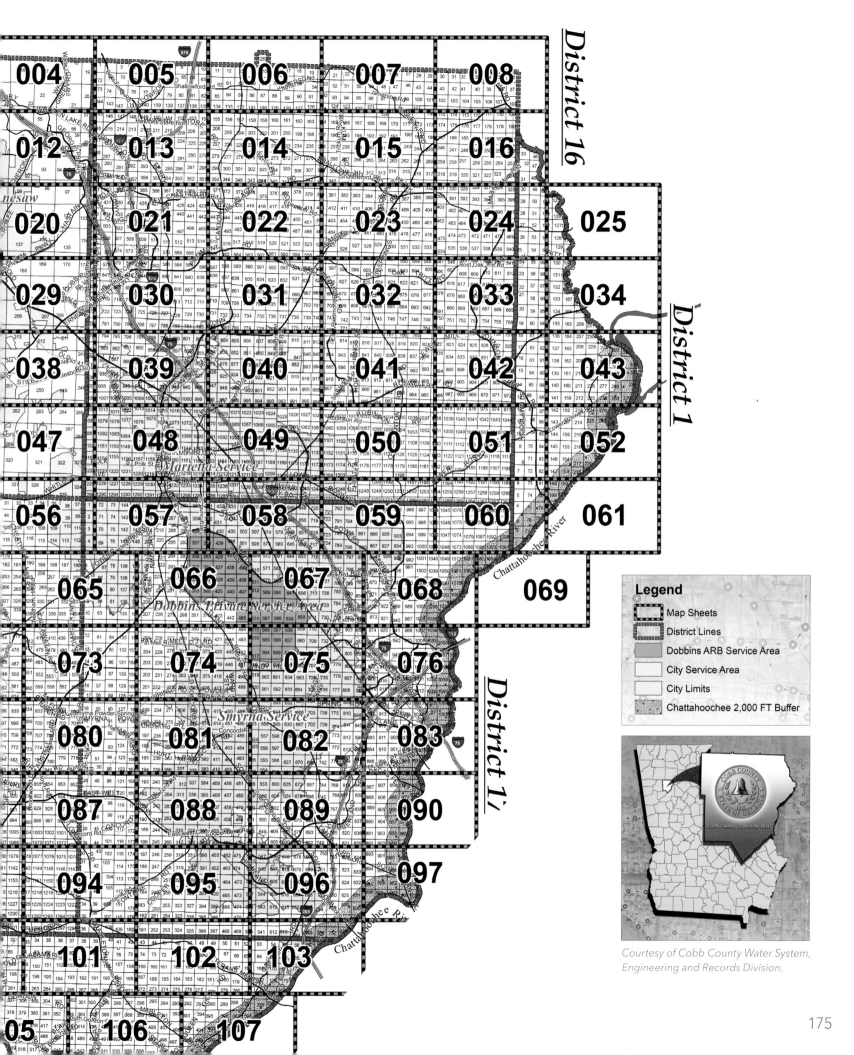

004 **005** **006** **007** **008**

012 **013** **014** **015** **016**

020 **021** **022** **023** **024** **025**

029 **030** **031** **032** **033** **034**

038 **039** **040** **041** **042** **043**

047 **048** **049** **050** **051** **052**

Marietta Service

056 **057** **058** **059** **060** **061**

Chattahoochee River

065 **066** **067** **068** **069**

Dobbins Private Service Area

073 **074** **075** **076**

080 **081** **082** **083**

Smyrna Service

087 **088** **089** **090**

094 **095** **096** **097**

101 **102** **103**

05 **106** **107**

Legend

⬚ Map Sheets

⬚ District Lines

▨ Dobbins ARB Service Area

▢ City Service Area

▢ City Limits

▨ Chattahoochee 2,000 FT Buffer

*Courtesy of Cobb County Water System,
Engineering and Records Division.*

MAPPING THE DISTRIBUTION OF WATER USE IN ILLINOIS

More than 1,300 communities in Illinois rely on different sources of water for municipal, industrial, and residential use. Sources of water throughout the state include Lake Michigan, inland surface waters such as rivers and reservoirs, groundwater, or a combination of sources. Communities may also purchase water from other communities or from public water distributors, which include private companies, water commissions, water districts, or water agencies.

This map depicts the complexity of where communities get their water and the network of water purchases throughout the state for the year 2012. Municipalities and public water distributors are color-coded according to the source of water they use. The purchase network depicts transactions between communities or public water distributors with arrows going from seller to purchaser.

Data for this map was gathered by the Illinois Water Inventory Program, which has tracked water use at high-capacity community wells and intakes (over 70 gallons per minute) throughout the state since 1979.

Illinois State Water Survey
Champaign, Illinois, USA
By Daniel R. Hadley, Joanna A. Krueger,
George S. Roadcap, and Conor R. Healy

CONTACT
Daniel R. Hadley
drhadley@illinois.edu

SOFTWARE
ArcGIS Desktop10.3.1

DATA SOURCES
US Geological Survey National Elevation Dataset,
National Hydrography Dataset Plus V2.1

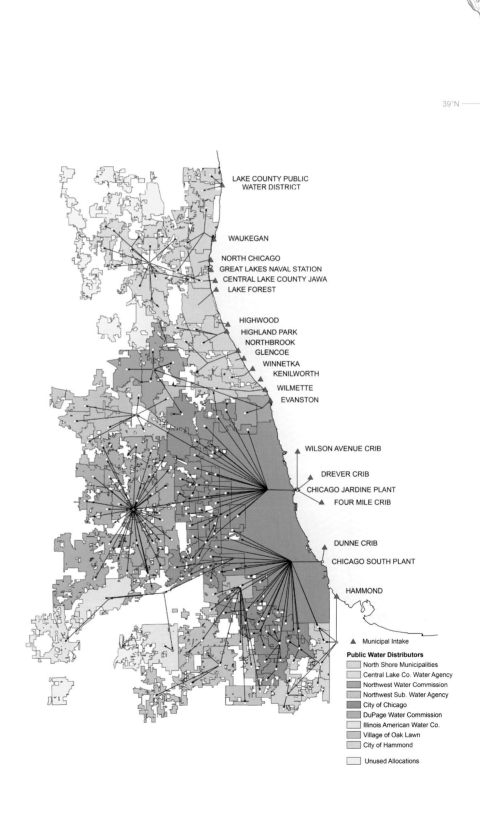

LAKE COUNTY PUBLIC WATER DISTRICT

WAUKEGAN

NORTH CHICAGO
GREAT LAKES NAVAL STATION
CENTRAL LAKE COUNTY JAWA
LAKE FOREST

HIGHWOOD
HIGHLAND PARK
NORTHBROOK
GLENCOE
WINNETKA
KENILWORTH
WILMETTE
EVANSTON

WILSON AVENUE CRIB

DREVER CRIB
CHICAGO JARDINE PLANT
FOUR MILE CRIB

DUNNE CRIB
CHICAGO SOUTH PLANT

HAMMOND

▲ Municipal Intake

Public Water Distributors
☐ North Shore Municipalities
☐ Central Lake Co. Water Agency
☐ Northwest Water Commission
☐ Northwest Sub. Water Agency
☐ City of Chicago
☐ DuPage Water Commission
☐ Illinois American Water Co.
☐ Village of Oak Lawn
☐ City of Hammond

☐ Unused Allocations

COTT

MORGAN

SANGAMON

Lake
Springfield

MACON

MOULTRIE

DOUGLAS

EDGAR

CHRISTIAN

COLES

GREENE

MACOUPIN

Lake
Shelbyville

SHELBY

CUMBERLAND

CLARK

MONTGOMERY

FAYETTE

EFFINGHAM

JASPER

CRAWFORD

JERSEY

39

MADISON

BOND

Carlyle
Reservoir

CLAY

LAWRENCE

MARION

RICHLAND

CLINTON

ST. CLAIR

WASHINGTON

WAYNE

EDWARDS

WABASH

Wabash River

MONROE

JEFFERSON

Rend Lake

RANDOLPH

PERRY

FRANKLIN

HAMILTON

WHITE

38°N

38°N

90°W

JACKSON

WILLIAMSON

SALINE

GALLATIN

88°W

Mississippi River

HARDIN

UNION

JOHNSON

POPE

Ohio River

ALEXANDER

PULASKI

MASSAC

37°N

89°W

Explanation of Symbols

— County Boundary

Major River | Stream

Lake | Reservoir

Purchase Network

○ Municipal Node

→ Water Purchase

Public Water Distributors

● Lake Michigan

○ Inland Surface Water

● Groundwater

● Mixed Source

Municipal Water Use

Lake Michigan

Inland Surface Water

Groundwater

Mixed Source

PUBLIC WATER SUPPLY

The United States, as a whole, withdrew from natural resources over 1,100 gallons of water per person every day in 2010 while the average household uses only about 130 gallons per capita per day (GPCD). Most households got those 130 gallons from a water utility provider and this map analyzes that publicly supplied water consumption state by state. Water provided to the public for use or purchase from utility organizations comprises about 12 percent of all water withdrawn from American natural resources with the remaining 88 percent mostly used for thermoelectric power and irrigation.

This map takes a wider look at the 12 percent provided by water utilities. PWCSA, which is a nonprofit water utility, needed to see how its customers' water consumption related to others in the country. The analysis shows that the western half of the United States relies more heavily upon publicly supplied water due to its lack of rainfall or groundwater resources. Additionally, irrigating even a quarter acre of land uses many times a normal household's typical water usage each day. This map clearly shows the divide between the less-agricultural and wetter east and the more-demanding and drier west and serves as a reminder that water use on a national level goes beyond what flows through one house's taps.

Prince William County Service Authority (PWCSA)
Woodbridge, Virginia, USA
By Jillian Rosche

CONTACT
Jillian Rosche
jrosche@pwcsa.org

SOFTWARE
ArcGIS Desktop10.3.1

DATA SOURCES
US Geological Survey Circular 1405,
US Census Bureau

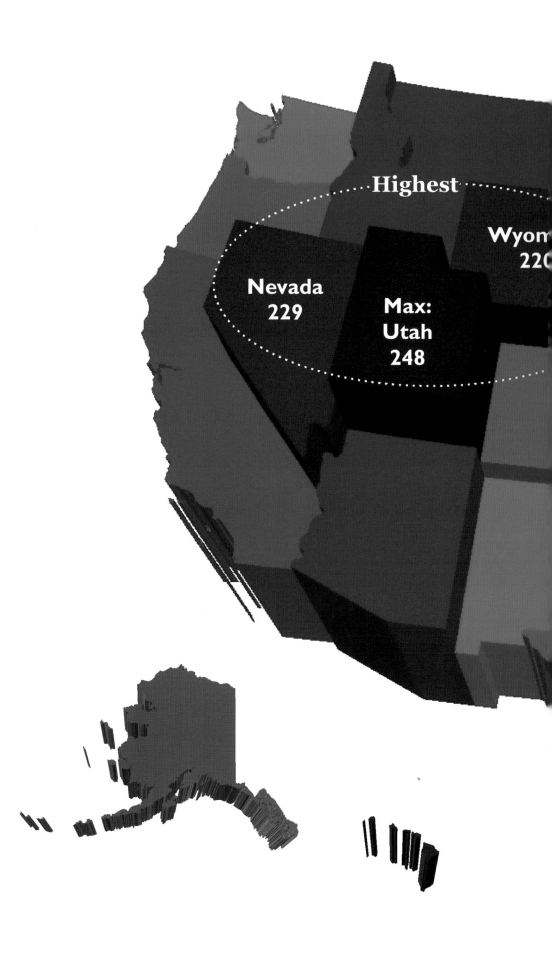

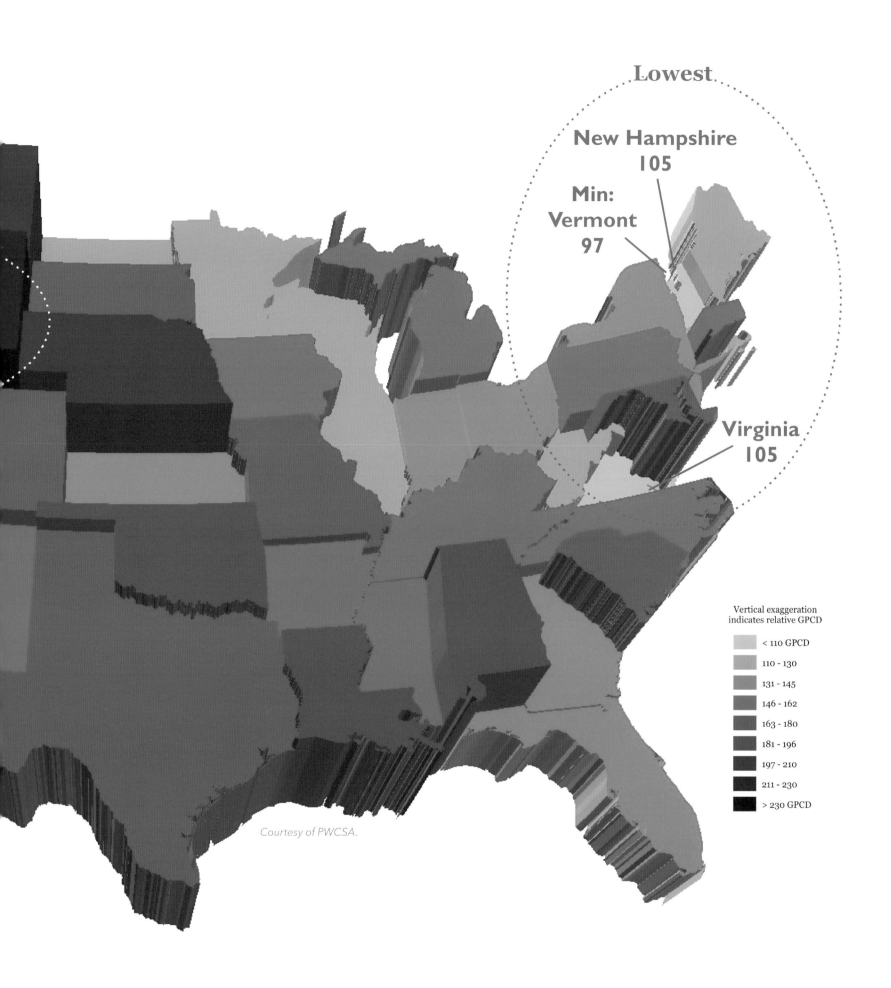

Lowest

New Hampshire
105

Min:
Vermont
97

Virginia
105

Vertical exaggeration
indicates relative GPCD

	< 110 GPCD
	110 - 130
	131 - 145
	146 - 162
	163 - 180
	181 - 196
	197 - 210
	211 - 230
	> 230 GPCD

Courtesy of PWCSA.

IS CLIMATE CHANGE AFFECTING YOUR WATER SYSTEM?

The City of Akron's public water system was established in 1880. Since 1953, Akron has been compiling water main break data that has become more accessible to track while demand to utilize this information has elevated. This map portrays a spatial analysis of 3,493 documented water main breaks on currently active water mains within the corporation limits of Akron. These breaks occurred during the city's winter "main break" season of November through February.

Water main break data was compared against temperature records to investigate if there's any correlation between suggested climate change and the increase in yearly water main breaks in Akron. Climate records from the region indicate that average daily temperatures during these cold weather months have increased slightly over this period while water main breaks have increased at a much higher rate.

While there is a correlation between these datasets, there are other influential factors that this analysis does not consider including age of pipe, pipe material, and soil conditions. Until Akron is better able to isolate the determining factors of water main breaks, city officials will have to continue to theorize as to the affects a warming climate has on the water system.

City of Akron
Akron, Ohio, USA
By Alex Bryan, Lucas Martin, and Wendy Doyle

CONTACT
Alex Bryan
abryan@akronohio.gov

SOFTWARE
ArcGIS Desktop 10.2.2

DATA SOURCES
City of Akron GIS, National Oceanic and Atmospheric Administration

Water Main Breaks

- Very Low (3 - 56)
- Low (56 - 109)
- Moderate (109 - 162)
- High (162 - 215)
- Very High (215 - 268)

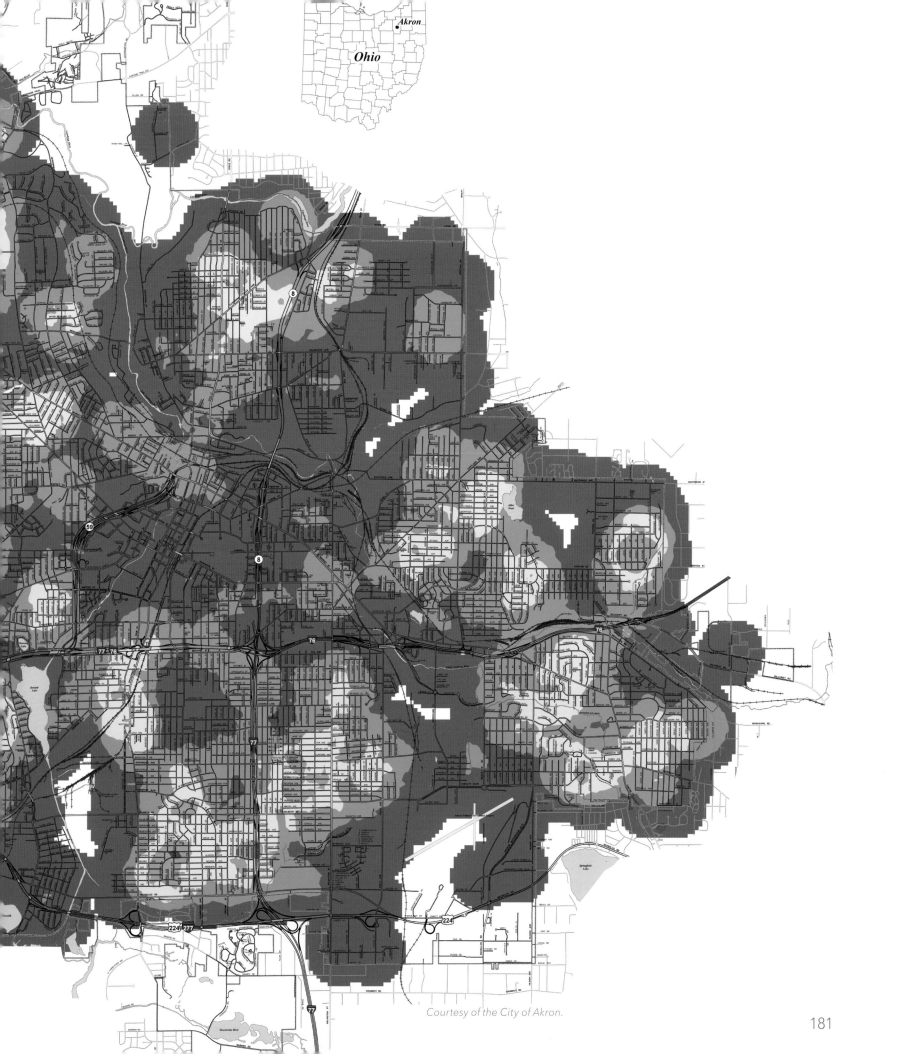

Courtesy of the City of Akron.

181

INDEX BY ORGANIZATION